THE MATURING OF THE ARTS ON THE AMERICAN CAMPUS: A COMMENTARY

by

JACK MORRISON

COLLEGE OF FINE ARTS

UNIVERSITY OF CALIFORNIA, LOS ANGELES

With a Foreword by

Clark Kerr

★ ★ ★ ★ ★ ★ ★

This study was funded in part and partially supported
by the American National Theater and Academy,
The Lilly Endowment and the UCLA College
of Fine Arts.

UNIVERSITY
PRESS OF
AMERICA

LANHAM • NEW YORK • LONDON

Copyright © 1985 by

University Press of America,® Inc.

4720 Boston Way
Lanham. MD 20706

3 Henrietta Street
London WC2E 8LU England

Library of Congress Cataloging in Publication Data

Morrison, Jack, 1912-
  The maturing of the arts on the American campus.

  Bibliography: p.
  1. Arts—Study and teaching (Higher)—United
States. I. Title.
NX303.M6 1985   700'.7'1173   85-7419
ISBN 0-8191-4709-5 (alk. paper)
ISBN 0-8191-4710-9 (alk. paper : pbk.)

All University Press of America books are produced on acid-free
paper which exceeds the minimum standards set by the National
Historical Publications and Records Commission.

To my friends and colleagues in the company of the arts in and out of academe whose dedication and talent have been at once a joy and a challenge to me.

Acknowledgments

This study was supported and partially funded by the American National Theater and Academy, the Lilly Endowment, and the UCLA College of Fine Arts. Their help was critical and graciously given.

If this book's main contribution is to the national dialogue in the field, it was developed most significantly from dialogue with my colleagues in the arts, particularly Robert H. Gray, Bernard Beckerman, Will Barnet, John Houseman, Bertil Lauritzen, W. McNeil Lowry, Claude Palisca, Norman Rice, Joseph Sloane, Roger Stevens, Michael Straight and John Straus. And, of course, the seminarians--but they speak for themselves in Chapter 2.

My good fortune in having Sondra Holwitz as editorial assistant is beyond counting. Her skill, judgment, and warm spirit are exemplary. In fund-raising and managing the seminar, Molly Maguire was insightful, effective and gracious. And my secretary, Lori Bowman, cracked the code of my crabbed handwriting with patience and accuracy seldom experienced.

Thanks also to McGraw-Hill for allowing me to reprint portions of Chapter 2 and Appendix F from my earlier volume, The Rise of the Arts on the American Campus, published in 1973.

But the man who started it all (by commissioning the first book fifteen years ago when he chaired the Carnegie Commission on Higher Education) and wrote the foreword for this current work is Clark Kerr whose interest and concern for the effective growth of the arts on campus is deep and abiding. It's thanks to his foresight that this serious contribution can be made.

Contents

Foreword

THE ARTS ON THE AMERICAN CAMPUS:
MATURING BUT STILL DIFFERENT

In 1973, the Carnegie Commission on Higher Education, which I chaired, published The Rise of the Arts on the American Campus by Jack Morrison. It told the fascinating story of the phenomenal increase in the study of the arts after World War II. Despite this increase, the arts, however, still then found themselves on the periphery of the campus-- still on the rise. More than a decade later--a short time in academic history--they are now said to be "accepted, even welcomed" on campus as Morrison reports in this new volume on The Maturing of the Arts on the American Campus.

The arts have now been added, permanently and securely, to the other great strains of intellectual and creative endeavors in American higher education. This is worth noting as a major advance in rounding out the scope of the higher learning--an advance that has gone too unnoticed for too long. First came the humanities which were at the center of the classical curriculum that began at Harvard in 1636. Second were added the sciences after 1800 (and the modern languages) which gave us the neoclassical curriculum. Then, third, came the great growth of the professional schools after the Civil War and, fourth, of the social sciences after 1900. All these combined to provide the modern curriculum. The arts have now been added, mostly since World War II, to create the contemporary "services society" curriculum (services society in the sense that a majority of the labor force is now employed in the services, not in the production of goods, category)-- with the arts as an increasingly important part of the services provided.

The arts are, I believe, even more accepted than this volume suggests. One of our Carnegie studies showed that 6 percent of all undergraduate majors in 1976 were in the arts. This would suggest a current total of 600,000 as against the 200,000 indicated here. (I realize there may be major discrepancies in the definitions used and in the sources of information). More remarkable, the percentage was 6 percent both in 1969 and in 1976 despite the enormous increase in the percentage for the professions--from 38 to 58 percent. The humanities and the social sciences were the great losers. In 1976, arts majors ranked in numbers in our study just above humanities majors and just below social science majors; and faculty members in the arts were 8 percent of all faculty.

The arts may at last be established but they are still different. My own experiences and a reading of this volume lead me to note some of these differences:

1.   The arts tend to be more divided internally against themselves than most (but not all) other fields. As this report notes: "The only points of resistance remaining are those in the arts themselves"--as stated by one university president. This was also the greatest area of resistance in the 1950s when, as Chancellor at Berkeley, I was trying to enlarge the area for the arts. The resistance came then, as now, from the historians and the critics versus those who create and perform--and it was sometimes bitter. I have concluded that the best solution is to keep the historians and critics in the College of Letters and Sciences, and split off the creators and the performers. The two groups do not mix well.

2.   The creative and performing arts do not fit well into the category of the academic disciplines. They are more like professional schools (or even teaching hospitals in the analogy of Eric Larrabee as reported in this volume). They may better be grouped in a College of Fine Arts such as I encouraged and helped establish 25 years ago at UCLA when I was president of the university; or, if large enough, have separate schools of their own. But they are a special kind of profession in that they are really many quite distinctive professions, not one; and in that few of these many professions are organized on the outside as they are in law and medicine and in most other fields. Thus there are usually no "standards" to be met before entering practice and less in the way of organized external support.

3.   It is more difficult to evaluate faculty performance in the arts than in most other fields because evaluation in the arts depends so much on taste and on personal judgment. The best statement I have seen on evaluation is the one included in this volume under the heading of "Review Policy." The arts, as compared particularly with the sciences, grow more horizontally or even centrifugally than they do vertically--with fewer tests of when progress has really been made. And, as this report

states: "Recruiting in the arts is not served well by paper."

4. Because of the difficulties in evaluation, the granting of tenure is more problemmatical. This is also so because artistic creativity in individuals is more likely to surge and decline than are the talents of those engaged in traditional scholarship. The arts are like professional sports, in this regard, with usually rather short periods of peak performance. This volume suggests greater than normal reliance on the employment of lecturers and on the use of medium-term contracts; and I agree. Schools of Architecture have traditionally relied heavily on part-time teaching personnel.

5. The arts must look in more directions than do most other areas of higher education: heavily to the non-majors (who may become what are called below "skilled amateurs") as well as to the majors; and heavily to public performance and exhibition as well as to teaching and creativeness. The first affects the content of the curricula ("the instructor is the curricula," as noted below) and the nature of the teaching; and the second affects both the orientation of and the specialized talents involved in administration. The arts have more obligations to all persons on the campus and in the surrounding community than do any other campus endeavors. Overall, administration is made more difficult by this complexity; so also is policy making by the faculty. The artistic temperament, in addition, does not lead to many "homeguard" types within the faculty to service the committee work and to render long-term loyalty to the institution. Arts faculties tend to more clusters of idiosyncratic individuals than communities of mutually supportive scholars.

6. The campus administration should be more a good patron than just the usual benevolent bureaucracy. Being a good patron is not easy. Historically, the best patrons have been wealthy aristocrats engaging their individual discriminative choices in competition with each other. Can benevolent bureaucracies ever be as effective?

7. The arts are one of the few areas within higher education which are bound to experience substantial growth. As America becomes more and more a nation of well-educated and affluent persons, the demand for knowledge of the arts and opportunities for enjoyment of them will also

continue to grow. The growth will be not only in quantity of demand but also in the quality of the expectations. The arts must demonstrate that they know how to grow effectively in both dimensions. This makes them different in degree from many other fields on campus where a more static future lies ahead.

Jack Morrison, once again, has performed a substantial service in describing and commenting upon the evolution of this fifth great stream of intellectual and creative endeavor within higher education in the United States as the arts mature on campus.

Clark Kerr
Berkeley, California
July 1984

1
Introduction

A maturing of the arts in higher education has begun within the last ten years. No longer do most academic administrators consider the arts as extra curricular affairs, as a kind of desirable or undesirable embellishment, which blooms or fades depending on the economic weather. And those in the arts can no longer enjoy a somewhat comforting paranoidal view that they are very special cases needing extra special attention. For the most part, the arts have matured to the point of becoming an accepted, even welcomed, young adult in the academic family.

As Clark Kerr suggests, there are five mainstreams in American higher education: the sciences, the social sciences, the humanities, the professions and, now, the creative arts. After conducting a follow-up study in longitudinal fashion of a selected group of diverse institutions of higher education, interviewing 80 or so educational leaders and convening a national seminar with leading experts in the fields, I agree with his assertions. It's clear to me that the ongoing development of the arts on the campus will continue to bloom or fade not depending on the economic weather but on the extent to which leaders in the arts and their colleagues achieve and demonstrate their maturity.

Longitudinal studies can be tedious and extraordinarily expensive. But this "follow-up study," ten years after the publication, The Rise of the Arts on the American Campus, (McGraw-Hill, 1973), with data collected in 1971 and 1972, provides an opportunity, from a longitudinal point-of-view, to establish benchmarks for the growth of the arts on campus over a decade or more. As the preface of that 1973 study for the Carnegie Commission in Higher Education states, "This study represents a frankly personal, though judicious, probe into the growth of the arts on campus by a participant in that growth." And that is what the current study does. It does not pretend to be "the definitive study of the arts in higher education." It does profess to make a contribution, in the

nature of informal, thoughtful commentary, to the understanding of a vital, significant portion of modern higher education. Nor does the current study encompass all of post-secondary education in the arts. (Conservatories like Juilliard,
the North Carolina School of the Arts, and the many proprietary schools are not included.) The study is restricted to
"higher education": the 2-year college; the 4-year liberal
arts col- lege; the comprehensive university; and the major
research university. The scope of this work is limited for
reasons of cost and time. It is not the author's intention to
ignore a very important portion of art training and education.

The National Association of State Universities & Land-
Grant Colleges (NASULC) and the American Council of Education
have made some preliminary efforts in the arts area, but the
scarcity of funds has limited their activities (see note 1).
The most promising effort at this writing is the HEADS project
(see note 2). HEADS has spent a great deal of time and
thought on taxonomy and nomenclature which are so vital to
data gathering. HEADS has launched the first comprehensive
study of the arts in higher education--at least as far as
numbers are concerned.

Pursuing a follow-up of the original seventeen institutions in the original study turned out to be less than satis-
factory. I quickly discovered that the economic crunch
(reduction-in-force and overload) had hampered my effort to
get current data that would be reliable enough to compare
effectively with the 1973 data. One top institution buffeted
the questionnaire like battledoor and shuttlecock among 5
offices until one administrator responded with a narrative
paragraph. He said the arts were thriving--and they are!
Another said that he would provide whatever information he
could provide "off the top." I saw that without a subvention
to pay for digging up the information, if it existed, I
wouldn't get any detailed response at all. Two major research
universities with the arts in a strong college which kept good
records provided data which was both reliable and useful.
"Institutional research" in the arts is almost non-existent.
Accordingly, I determined to put more reliance on the
"national seminar" and interviews.

The response to the 1983 questionnaire was nonetheless
useful in molar terms. They did make it clear that the arts
continue to operate on 16 of those campuses; that their
budgets did increase; that, on the whole, they suffered
conditions no better and no worse than the other disciplines

on campus. For these reasons, I moved my method from its original basic reliance in the follow-up of the 1973 questionnaire to an increased dependency on the seminar and the interviews. Therefore my method invoked "participant observation." (James A. Robinson considered this method in his review of James L. Fisher's new book, Power of the Presidency, in Change (16,5-1984). He saw "'participant observation' reviving as a serious research method among scholars turned leaders.") Whether this is a scholarly euphemism for good journalism or not, it describes the method I turned to under pressure of reality of the forces I found under the constraints of time and money. All administrators face decision-making with minimal data all the time anyway. Accordingly, I cannot endorse avoiding the issues of the day in the arts because there is not enough "hard data" to fit textbook experimental design.

The aim of this book, then, is to offer some good information and a few useful benchmarks on the growth of the arts in higher education over the last ten years. Such information will be helpful to chief academic officers in higher education who are from other academic fields and need some guidance as well as to deans, chairs of departments, university committees, and boards of trustees or regents. The concerned layman with an interest in the arts may find useful information as well as students of higher education and staff personnel on the campus.

The most striking change encountered by this writer in visiting various campuses today is that the arts, at least among administrators, is thoroughly accepted as an integral part of the academic scene. (For a listing of those interviewed, see Appendix A.) At the faculty level on the campus, and among department chairs, there is reasonable doubt. But for presidents, chief academic officers and deans, there is no question that the arts are one of the established curricula on campus. As one university president put it, the only points of resistance remaining are those in the arts themselves. It's as if some of the arts faculty can't take "yes" for an answer. Although there may be some holdouts on the "legality" of the arts in academe on some campuses, the factor holding up developments in the arts lies "not in the stars, Dear Brutus, but in ourselves."

For further consideration of the rationale for the arts being on campus, the reader is referred to Chapter 1 of the original volume, "The Case for the Arts in Higher Education." Assuming the case has been made, what has happened over the last decade and what appears to lie ahead? What lies down the road in the 80s and 90s and beyond?

Chapter 2 begins with the original (1973) historical sketches reprinted here for your review. Then, authorities in the field offer updates for each of the disciplines and share a point-of-view about the current condition of each art and a likely look toward future developments. In these articles, a positive stance is noted, indicating that a maturity of the arts on campus is underway.

Appendix B offers updates of the "Profiles of Selected Colleges and Universities." Chapter 4 of the original volume carries the earlier profile study and readers may compare (see note 3) and contrast any changes made during the intervening years. The profiles indicate the growth over the decade and further buttresses the view that the arts on campus are now an integral part of the academic scene. Again, there is no intention to offer the profiles as "hard" statistical evidence of the state of the arts on campus. For example, any attempt to draw averages from these profiles would be foolhardy. The number is too small, the variations in campuses and their programs too great, and labeling (taxonomy) is too disparate. The "Profiles," then, should be treated as "rough notes." They do, however, give some useful information "in media res" for this young field in its maturing phases. They are offered as a help to academic administrators and others, who, like administrators everywhere, must constantly make timely spot-decisions with minimal data (see note 4). Therefore, while more good information is being unearthed and the amount of "hard data" increased, the problem is to use what information we do have wisely rather than complain about the lack of more data. That's a cop-out.

There is no chapter on national statistics as there was in the first volume. Some statistical data are provided in Appendix D, but there is even less information now than there was fifteen years ago. To repeat an old theme, there should be more "hard data" developed over the years, and HEADS is making an effort to do this. The departments of "Institutional Research" are beginning to deal with the arts, especially at the larger schools, but those in the arts must prevail upon their administrations to develop institutional research in the arts--and in ways which will be useful. For example, surveying the small liberal arts college with the same instrument as the major research university is obviously absurd. And developing an appropriate number for each classification of institution (probably four: 2-year community college, 4-year liberal arts college, comprehensive university and major research university) takes personnel, time and money. Fortunately, the International Council of Fine Arts Deans is concerned with this problem and, along with "HEADS," is pursuing it with vigor.

In Chapter 3, "Seminar Results," provides findings drawn from the sketches, profiles, the summary of a national seminar on the arts in higher education, and site-visits to the selected colleges and universities as well as interviews with authorities in the arts (see note 5). The evidence for considering the field to be a maturing phase is reviewed. Chapter 4 offers discussion, observations and recommendations concerning vital issues at stake in the maturing process.

The appendices provide additional information about resistance to the arts, earned degrees, educational data, national norms, data on American graduate students and the text of the questionnaire.

Notes

1 Let it be noted here that the time is ripe for a full-blown, well-funded survey of post-secondary education in the arts in all its manifestations. Our society is more deeply involved in it than it knows.

2 The Higher Educations Arts Data Service, Reston, Virginia

3 Morrison (1973)

4 This is a general problem for management which deserves some serious attention. Putting off decisions "until we have more information" may be an appropriate response in a given situation at a given time. But not making a decision, despite the paucity of data, may be catastrophic. Understanding this problem is particularly important to the arts simply because they are so new on campus and little "hard data" exists. But "hard data," desirable as it may be, is not necessarily a requirement for useful information which contributes to thought and action. Darwin's basic information for developing his theory of evolution appeared in his book, a travelog, called, The Voyage of the Beagle. It was "merely anecdotal," of course, but the impact on thinking and action in the modern world has been enormous.

5 The names of those interviewed are published in Appendix A.

2
Historical Sketches and Updates

Members of the National Seminar on the Arts and three others from their fields were invited to review the 1973 sketches (see note 6) and make any personal commentary and forecast of things to come. The invitation urged the writers to write as they might in a personal essay--not to write as a pundit, but simply to express a personal viewpoint. Each commentary follows the original sketches, *which are printed in italics*. This allows the reader to look for trends and review his own perception of the field. In any case, the updates of the sketches indicate that the arts on the American campus are an integral part of the academic world and reflect a broad, deeply felt, concern to make them more effective. The growth of the arts had not crested in 1973 when the original essays were published. Earlier speculation and a need for better forecasting inspired a need for this updated volume.

If we look back into history we see the arts--in different places and in different ways--moving from the periphery to the heart of the campus and infiltrating the curriculum. A separate look at each of the arts during the course of their infiltration gives a sense of how this developed, documents the growth, and provides a historical base for the current scene and some appreciation of the rate of change. Because theater and dance drew somewhat more attention and certainly more invective than art and music, sketches of their development are given first. Note in the rise of all of the arts an increasing involvement on the campus at the turn of the century, a noticeable acceleration between the two world wars, and a strong upsurge after World War II, particularly around 1960.

Notes

6 See Morrison (1973). This material was reprinted by permission of McGraw-Hill Book Company.

THEATER   Some interest in the drama was present at Harvard at the end of the seventeenth century, as President Increase Mather made a note in his diary on October 10, 1698, that he had "examined the Scholars about the comedy, etc." A "pastoral colloquy" in 1702 at William and Mary and a performance in 1736 by "the young gentlemen of the Colledge" of "the tragedy of Cato" are generally considered to be the first dramatic performances by American college students. But criticism of plays was also present in this period. Writing to the Overseers of Harvard College in 1723, Cotton Mather expressed an attitude which was to be held by many in the next 250 years:

"Whether the scholars have not their studies filled with books which may truly be called Satan's Library. Whether the books mostly read among them are not plays, novels, empty and vicious pieces of poetry" (Quincy, 1860, vol. I, p. 559). State and church would repeatedly band together to keep these satanic forces in check.

To be sure, a case had been made for the theater in England by William Gager, the Christ College dramatist who answered an attack by Dr. John Rainolds of Owen College in 1592. Gager (Boas, 1914, pp. 235-36, 241) responded with a rationale that braved the Atlantic crossing and is still used today.

We contrarwise doe it [produce plays] to recreate owre selves, owre House, and the better part of the Vniversitye, with some learned Poem or other; to practyse owre owne style eyther in prose or verse; to be well acquantyed with Seneca or Plautus . . . your goodwill I doe and ever will most gladly embrace, and your judgment toe, in this cause so farr, as you wryte in the generall agaynst Histriones.

Gager's argument for theater on the educational grounds that it fosters the development of individual talent and imparts knowledge of the great works of the past continues to be the basic rationale for all the arts on the campus today.

The diary kept by Nathaniel Ames of Harvard in 1761 indicates increased interest in plays. He notes seeing Cato performed twice in July of 1758, seeing The Orphan the following year, and playing in The Recruiting Officer himself that year. In 1765, however, Ames enters this note: "Scholars punished at College for acting over the great and last day in

*a very shocking manner, personating the Jude eterat Devil,
etc." (Matthews, 1914, p. 295).*

The drama appeared in the forms of "academical exercises," extracurricular endeavor, and playwriting by faculty
and students for commencements and "dialogues." Apparently
there was some lessening of interest in the early part of the
nineteenth century, or perhaps drama was attracting less
attention, but activities in theater continued. By 1844 the
Hasty Pudding Club at Harvard had emerged. It was described
as "a rather jolly amalgam of literary, convivial, and patri-
otic elements" and "theatrical representations," and it served
as a prototype for the development of extracurricular dramatics in other colleges and universities.

Harvard's historian, Samuel Eliot Morison, observed that
"from the Civil War to the World War, Harvard undergraduates
had an insatiable thirst for theatricals." This enthusiasm,
moreover, was not restricted to the Harvard campus, but
developed in extracurricular productions all over the country.
The expansion of the railroad brought professional companies
to campuses and communities in all quarters of the country.
The "musical burlesque," written and staged by clubs, gave a
currency to a kind of populist theater. Language faculties
began to sponsor foreign language classics. This was the
period when "the Greek play" became an annual, carefully
prepared event on many campuses.

Soon the theater was respectable enough for universities
to invite professionals for lectures. Steele MacKaye appeared
at Princeton in the 1870s, lecturing on "The Mystery of
Emotion and its Expression in Art." Henry Irving was at
Harvard in 1884-85 and Joseph Jefferson was at the University
of Michigan in 1897. By the turn of the century, or about 200
years after plays were considered at Harvard as part of
"Satan's Library," hostility to theater had been allayed, and
acted drama was eyeing a place in the sanctity of the
curriculum.

Thomas Dickinson gave a short-lived course on the
"staging of plays" at Baylor in 1901-02, but George Pierce
Baker is generally credited as the first American professor to
be concerned with "living theater." In a personal note to the
author, Kenneth Macgowan wrote:

Baker gave his playwriting course, first at Radcliffe, in the spring of 1904. He did not give it

*at Harvard until the spring of 1906. The 47 Work-
shop also began at Radcliffe. The first performance, directed by Sam Hume, while Baker was in
Europe, was in January, 1913. It was made possible
by the Radcliffe 47 Club, which raised $500. Eng-
lish 47 did not teach anything about the physical
production of plays, though Baker may have mentioned
the differences between the playhouses and methods
of various periods.*

*In 1925 when Baker left the Harvard 47 Workshop to set up a
new department of drama at Yale, New York columnist Heywood
Broun wrote:*

>   YALE   47
>   HARVARD   0

*"Bootlegging" of theater into the curriculum character-
ized most of the growth of theater in higher education through
World War II. Public Speaking 2 a-b, for example, was often a
euphemism for "acting." The next step was an omnibus "play
production" course deemed necessary for theater training.
Exceptions to this included the drama department at Carnegie
Institute of Technology (began in 1914), Alexander Drummond's
work at Cornell, the theater concentration in speech at
Northwestern, and E.C. Mabie's program at Iowa University.*

*In 1936 in St. Louis, Mabie organized the American
Educational Theatre Association (AETA-now the American Theatre
Association) as a separate section of the National Association
of Teachers of Speech. Mabie had also been a key figure in
the development of the National Theatre Conference (founded in
1931, reorganized with membership limited in 1936), which
encouraged foundation support for college and community
theaters. By 1949, AETA had developed the talent, experience,
and funds to launch its own major publication, the Educational
Theatre Journal. Thus, at the midpoint of the twentieth
century, the theater in colleges and universities may be said
to have established itself on its own terms. Diversity and
functionalism still existed, but the theater had brought
itself into academe in the short 250 years since President
Mather's diary entry of 1698.*

*In 1960 AETA published for the first time the Directory
of American College Theatre, edited by Burnet Hobgood. In
1967 Richard Ayers brought out a second edition, which is the
most recent overview of the field. He reports that of 1,581
regionally accredited United States colleges and universities,*

30 percent (574) offer degrees in theater as a field of study. Although the data are only partially complete, an annual audience of approximately 5 million witnesses to 10,000 reported productions is indicated. There were 116,000 enrolled students in formal classrooms and another 100,000 students involved in putting on plays. Of the schools offering these programs 43 percent describe themselves as providing a liberal arts education and 10.5 percent attest to liberal arts training with a vocational bent. Another 43 percent describe their motives as recreational and avocational and 3.5 percent classify them as professional-commercial.

In the seven years between the first and second editions of the *Directory* (from 1960 to 1967), the number of undergraduate majors tripled from about 5,500 to 18,000 and the number of courses offered for credit increased from 7,000 to 12,000. In 1967 there were 168 institutions offering the master's degree and 38 offering the doctorate. Since 1960 twenty more programs at the graduate level have been added. About 3,000 graduate degrees were awarded each year between 1960 and 1967.

At present, many efforts are underway to raise the standards of work in the field and to "professionalize" certain programs. A division of the American Theatre Association, the University Repertory Theatre Association, has sprung up to develop graduate theater companies and to professionalize them at the grass roots level. The League for Professional Theatre Training, composed of 11 institutions, is more selective and emphasizes high-quality work. These are manifestations of deep concern that college theater should have a closer liaison with the professional theater, a view strongly stated by both professionals and academic theater men in a special 1966 issue of the *Educational Theatre Journal*, "The Relationship Between Educational Theatre and Professional Theatre."

Another development is the emergence of a small, but forceful group of younger faculty who are concerned with a wider use of theater at all levels of education. Plays, traveling troupes, curricular materials, and teacher training for grades kindergarten through 12 are being developed for the classroom teacher and the orchard-run of children, as well as for the talented and motivated student.

From its center--the liberal arts, avocational base of most offerings in higher education--the field, then, is moving in two directions: (1) toward the professionalizing of work at *the highest levels of artistry in both established and experimental areas and (2) toward the professionalizing of theater education for the schools, kindergarten through twelfth grade (Graham, 1966).*

A development in the experimental area which appears likely to influence the field is that which is sometimes called "anthropological theater," a mode which is closer to dance. It is based on an approach to theater in its fundamental, ritualistic relationships to man's daily life and expressive behavior. "Political theater" and "street theater" are current manifestations. Some young practitioners of the arts are currently of the view that they will never return to the formal or traditional theater. Whatever the outcome, groups such as the Bread and Puppet Theater based at Goddard College are the antithesis of "elitist theater" as seen in conventional buildings of the establishment on the campus. These groups are likely to bring the theater closer to the more intimate, humanized experience which the "primitive ring" used to provide for tribal events. At the same time, an effort to create a similar, personalized encounter with theater by means of technology and multimedia is also at work. Hopefully, the campus will provide a receptive, useful laboratory not only for experiment in form and technique, but also for free play of expressive behavior in the theater which reflects the hopes, passions, and problems of our society.

Notes

Note: In this section on theater I relied heavily on Wallace (1954); particularly John L. Clark's chapter, "Educational Dramatics in Nineteenth Century Colleges" (pp. 521-551); and Clifford Eugene Hamar's chapter, "College and University Theatre Instruction in the Early Twentieth Century" (pp. 572-594).

THEATER
(Updated)

After two decades of expansionism in theater education signified chiefly by the proliferation of Bachelor or Fine Arts and Master of Fine Arts degree programs and by the building of arts complexes on campuses, the brakes have been applied as an outgrowth of Reaganomics, federal and state legislative conservatism, and tight-money policies among campus administrations.

What happened in those two expansionist decades of the 1960s and 1970s forecast in The Carnegie Commission on Higher Education study entitled The Rise of the Arts on the American Campus (Morrison, 1973)? There have been five principal developments: (a) Theater degree granting programs at all levels of education proliferated; (b) Performing arts high schools received an imprimatur from the profession and Boards of Education (there are now 200 across the country); (c) The MFA became widely accepted as a terminal degree in performance; (d) Ph.D. degree programs flagged under the popularity of the MFA among students and performance faculties; (e) Professional theaters and guest artist programs emerged on campuses as facets of training programs. It is the latter phenomenon that I wish to address, for the emergence of the professional theater on campus has created a watershed in theater arts: the dividing line separates theater education for the amateur as opposed to conservatory training for the professional.

Theater education began in America as a means of artistic expression for the amateur. In the eighteenth century, college students imitating their British cousins performed classical plays on campuses as early as the first quarter of the century. A "pastoral colloquy" in 1702 at William and Mary and a performance of "the tragedy of Cato" in 1736 are generally considered to be the first dramatic performances by American college students.

The argument for theater on educational grounds (literally on the campus) was based upon the well-worn idea that theatrical performance fostered the development of individual talent and impacted knowledge of the great works of the past on the minds of the present. This continues to be the basic rationale for theater arts on campus today.

But the coming of the Space Age in the 1960s and the

Computer Age in the 1980s has likewise impacted our thinking about the role of the arts in higher education. The age of the trained professional does not accommodate theater as an extra-curricular activity, or the "bootlegging" of theater courses in Speech and English curriculums. The B.A. degree in theater arts is now accepted as part and parcel of an array of choices within a liberal arts education. According to the American Theater Association's directory of college theater programs, there are currently over 1,600 programs producing theater and awarding degrees.

But the field that was merrily proliferating degree programs (both graduate and undergraduate), as well as arts complexes in the 60s and 70s, has taken a quantum leap in the last ten years analogous to the emergence (on university campuses) of the computer specialist, his hardware and software packages, computer centers and instructional programs. While the liberal arts as the avocational base of most theater arts offerings in higher education is taken for granted today, the big push is toward the professionalizing of training (toward a quality of excellence) at the highest levels of artistry in both established and experimental areas. The direction was originally charted by the founding of the League of Professional Theater Training Programs (in 1971), now composed of 13 institutions (see note 7). The League, as the organization is called, is a selective, self-monitoring group representing the highest quality of training in the field. A second group, the University/Resident Theater Association (URTA) composed of 42 member theater programs, was devised to encourage the use of guest artist contracts on campus and to recruit university-age students to form companies on campus for purposes of training and quality performance. Parallel to the emergence of the League and URTA among our most prestigious theater training institutions, we find as university-sponsored entities the emergence of professional theater operating under League of Resident Theaters (LORT), guest artist, or Equity letter of agreement contracts.

Access to the professional theater and its working professionals is the new wrinkle in the whole cloth of theater education for the next decades. The merger represents business, curricular, and artistic priorities on the campus. Nor does this trend represent "elitist" theatre as opposed to "populist" liberal arts education. The phenomenon is a response of theater educators/artists to the demands of the computer age for training the professional to utilize the tools of his or her craft. The LORT theater on campus--a resident professional theater operating under the Resident Theater Agreement of Actors Equity--has become the rising symbol of this new philosophy of training the theater professional. For some it represents the apprentice period for the Actors Equity card; for others, networking with proven professionals; for all, it is the proving ground for one's professional training and the testing ground for one's ability to survive as a professional among professionals.

Like the University museum or library, the professional theater as an integral part of the university campus and higher education is a distinct sign of our times. The computer age requires specialized training in the craft (with its tools of organization) in an educational milieu questing for survival and excellence in the 1980s. The most popular book on The New York Times book chart for 38 weeks has been In Search of Excellence: Lessons from America's Best-Run Companies (Harper & Row, 1982) by Thomas J. Peters and Robert H. Waterman, Jr.--lessons not overlooked by theater educators. The quest for excellence among the structures of America's corporations is mirrored in the current watershed in theater education. The results are threefold: (1) acceptance of theater arts as a liberal arts component (a 250-year-old labor); (2) a moratorium on the creation of new graduate programs and a rethinking of the Ph.D. degree in a performing art; (3) a concern for professionalism in training and performance.

In the 1960s a few were arguing that college theater programs should develop a closer liaison with professional theaters. In 1966, The Educational Theater Journal published a special issue on "The Relationship Between Educational Theater and Professional Theater." Both academic and professional theater people argued in this issue for a closer liaison of college theater programs with the professional theater. This goal has now been made concrete with the location of LORT theaters on campus (see note 8). (See Figure 1.)

To use the language of America's successful corporate executives, there is good news. The best of theater training for the young professional is not to be found wholly within British and European companies. The theater training program associated with the professional theater (and its larger, national network of LORT theaters) is our new model for training.

There are, of course, major economic considerations dealing with scale of operation of such a holistic program and questions about our ability to achieve results (especially quality) by mingling young and established professionals. But one economic advantage, it is argued, is the merger of public and private monies in support of the endeavor. While general audiences support the university-based theater--long a part of student's liberal education--today corporations, businesses, and foundations fund these theaters along with federal and state arts agencies. We've come a long way since George Pierce Baker's 47 Workshop at Harvard in 1913. Since the establishment of formal degree granting programs in the 1920s, the campus has provided theaters as useful laboratories for experiments in form and technique and as spaces for free play of expressive behavior in production and performance.

Again, the times and models have changed radically. In the 1980s, the campus has proved hospitable to the corporate professional structure in response to a society troubled by inflation, conservative economic policies, social problems, and world conflict. The movement of professional theater to the campus is one response of the theater educator to the university's corporate-thinking. It is a sign of the times and an avenue to the future of theater arts in higher education.

Milly S. Barranger
The University of North
Carolina, Chapel Hill

Notes

7   The American Conservatory Theater, Boston University, Brandeis University, Carnegie-Mellon University, The Juilliard School, New York University, North Carolina School of the Arts, Southern Methodist University, State University of New York at Purchase, Temple University, University of California at San Diego, University of Washington, Yale School of Drama.

8   At the time of this writing, there are nine such theaters located on university campuses: Yale Repertory Theater, American Repertory Theater (Harvard), McCarter Theater (Princeton), Syracuse Stage, Asolo State Theater of Florida (FSU), PlayMakers Repertory Company (University of North Carolina, Chapel Hill), Missouri Repertory Theater (University of Missouri, Kansas City), Repertory Theater of St. Louis (Webster College), The Clarence Brown Company (University of Tennessee, Knoxville).

FIGURE 1. The Paul Green Theatre. Opened in 1981 on the campus of the University of North Carolina, Chapel Hill. A thrust stage, seating 504, the Paul Green Theatre is one of two theaters operated by Playmakers Repertory Company and the Department of Dramatic Art.

DANCE   Dance, it turns out, was not thought to be all bad by the founders of New England. In 1625, before coming to Massachusetts from England, the Reverend John Cotton wrote:

> *Dancing (yea through mixt) I would not simply con-*
> *demn. For I see two sorts of mixt dancings in use*
> *with God's people in the Old Testament, the one*
> *religious, Exod. XV, 20, 21; the other civil, tend-*
> *ing to the praise of conquerors, as the former of*
> *God, I. Sam. XVII, 6, 7. Only lascivious dancing to*
> *wanton ditties, and amorous gestures and wanton*
> *dalliances, expecially after feasts, I would bear*
> *witness against, as a great flabella libidinis (in*
> *Marks, 1957, p.15).*

In 1628, William Bradford attacked the Maypole, calling it a "stynching idol" around which heathens worshipped. But early theorists of education in England such as Sir Thomas Elyot in 1531, John Milton in Tracate on Education in 1644, and John Locke in Some Thoughts Concerning Education in 1690, saw dance as part of education. Locke wrote:

> *Dancing, being that which gives graceful Motions all*
> *the Life, and above all things Manliness, and a*
> *becoming Confidence to Young Children, I think*
> *cannot be learned too early...it gives Children*
> *manly Thought and Carriage, more than any thing*
> *(ibid., p.17).*

In 1687, an instructor at Harvard wrote in Compendium Physicae that, despite abuse by man's corruption, the gymnastic arts, which include dancing, were invented and taught for the regulating of poise.

In Virginia, dancing was prohibited on the Sabbath, but proponents of aristocratic education expected a gentleman to dance well. In Philadelphia in 1706, the Society of Friends agreed that "Friends are generally grieved that a dancing and fencing school are tolerated in this place." The Shakers, however, who arrived in this country near the beginning of the Revolutionary War, had definite dance patterns as part of their worship. Others considered dance to be part of their children's education. The Kent County School in Chestertown, Maryland, advertised in 1745 that "young gentlemen may be instructed in fencing and dancing by very good masters" as well as being taught Greek, Latin, writing, and arithmetic. Thomas Jefferson scheduled dancing for his daughter from ten o'clock to one o'clock every day, and President Edward Holyoke of Harvard College noted in his diary that he had paid a Mr. Turner for dancing lessons for his daughter Peggy. Plain people and blacks danced for the fun of it at bees and frolics.

Despite this evident interest in dancing in the eighteenth century, however, there was a movement toward the end of that century and into the nineteenth by leaders in higher education and the church to keep dancing off the campus, as well as out of commencement and other college exercises. This effort was sustained by such forces as the Great Revival of 1858, during which tracts appeared under such titles as "The Social Evils of Dancing, Card Playing, and Theatre-Going." In general, this spirit kept dance out of colleges and universities throughout the nineteenth century, but it was always a seesaw battle and, in some places, dance was encouraged and developed. Harvard had licensed a dancing school in 1815, and Jefferson had suggested that dance be included in the curriculum at the University of Virginia because it was one of the arts that "embellished life." The University of North Carolina banned any dancing. William and Mary followed the more liberal views of English colleges and maintained that the college had to offer dance if it were to compete with English schools for the education of aristocratic gentlemen. President Moses Wadell of the University of Georgia banished dance, but it quickly returned on his retirement.

Dance began to appear as a form of exercise in private schools. Emma Willard brought dance into Middlebury College and later into her Troy Female Seminary. Catherine Beecher introduced it at the Hartford Female Seminary, as did Mary Lyon at Mount Holyoke Seminar. In each case, dance was part of an exercise program. The nose of the camel under the tent of respectability was the act of providing music for "light calisthenics." In 1869, Matthew Vassar told his board of trustees at Vassar College, "I heartily approve of [dancing]." The period after the Civil War saw further incorporation of dance into schools and colleges as part of physical education.

The do-si-do between dance and American higher education continued until 1917, when Margaret D'Houbler drove a salient into the fields of academe with an educational concept of dance as art, no longer limited to recreational and "genteel" social exercises. After studying with professionals in New York, Miss D'Houbler returned to the University of Wisconsin in 1917 with the idea of teaching a truly educational dance form and offered the first program in dance as an art experience. By 1926 the university had approved the first major dance curriculum, and dance had caught on in academe. By 1948, Walter Terry reported that at least 105 colleges and universities offered dance and that 92 gave academic credit for it. In 1969, the National Dance Division of the American Association of Health, Physical Education, and Recreation reported that 110 institutions gave a major or concentration on dance. Of these, 22 were in separate departments, 6 in theatre, 5 in fine arts, and 77 in physical education--the trend being away from physical education toward identification of dance as such. Forty-two institutions offered the master's degree and six the doctorate. In 1962, New York University awarded the first Ph.D. for choreography as a performing art. The "dissertation" was presented in concert form.

An important aspect of this growth was the close relationship that grew up in the 1930s between higher education and New York professionals, particularly Hanya Holm, Charles Weidman, Doris Humphrey, Martha Graham, and Louis Horst. Bennington College, with Martha Hill at the helm, gave direction to efforts to use the talents of mature artists throughout the country, and the world of education today continues to be injected with the drive of the professional world. This healthy relationship was emphasized and encouraged by a Developmental Conference on the Dance sponsored by the Arts and Humanities Program of the U.S. Office of Education in 1968 (Dance . . ., 1968). The result of combined professional and academic effort is that offerings in the schools now include techniques (various modern styles, ballet, and jazz) at all levels, extensive courses in choreography, repertory, rhythmic training, music for dance, music ethnic forms, notation, aesthetics, theory and philosophy, history, theater, dance therapy, methods teaching, and dance for children. Twelve states now recognize a special teaching certificate for dance in their public schools.

Research in dance has been supported by private and federal grants, and the Committee on Research on Dance (CORD) has held five conferences. The Dance Collection of the New York Public Library in Lincoln Center has become the most significant repository for dance in the world. One result of the concern for and study of what some people call the oldest art form is that folk dancing, taught by rote as "exercises" in the twenties, is now taught as dance in terms of folk art and ethnic arts, as expressive of cultures. Indeed, Alan Lomax's current worldwide research in "choreometrics" finds that cultures may be identified by their dance forms.

As the newest of the arts to be included in higher education, dance has been less concerned than the others with academic partitioning and territorial prerogatives and is developing its genuine concerns with society as well as developing itself as a rigorous art form. Since 1959, in the company of the other arts as a constituent member of the National Council of the Arts in Education (now the American Council for the Arts in Education), dance has championed the right of each human being to experience art in some form compatible with his interests and abilities. In fact, many consider dance and film not only as forms which are in current vogue, but also as forms which are strongly contributing to the revitalization of the arts on campus today.

Notes

Note: This section on dance is based on an unpublished manuscript by Dorothy Madden (1972), chairman of the department of dance at the University of Maryland, and America Learns to Dance, by Joseph E. Marks, III (1957).

DANCE
(Updated)

Dance is very much alive, well, living in the U.S.A., and spilling over into Europe. In fact, dance is on a crest, surging. The number of programs in higher education have doubled since The Rise of the Arts on the American Campus was published in 1973. Important organizations supporting, nurturing, and shaping the growth of dance have appeared: Congress on Dance Research, Council of Dance Administrators, The National College Festival Performances in Washington D.C., The National Association of Schools of Dance. Literature and criticism of dance join the boom. The effect of the touring program has woven professional dance and dance in education into bright happenings--another boom.

Perhaps it actually is an advantage rather than the reverse to have been away from the states for a period of time, for one returns like a visitor to a scene already known, rather like Our Town. One hears old words with new overtones, sees new faces alive with commitment, is aware of new energies attacking familiar problems, and great spirit abounds. Although much has changed and advanced, much is the same. The core is present and solid. The scene does not seem so much a watershed (in dance) to me as it does a crest which we must learn to ride--at the same time to be wary in that riding.

Having noted the happy fact of the explosion...the boom ...let me lower the boom. We need to point out the temper, timbre, and terror of the times: recession, cuts in budget (inviting problems of faculty morale), the NEA cut in the touring program, disbanded dance companies, programs in dance which have been cut or absorbed into other departments, and computer charisma. I am aware that we walk the razor's edge. Dance is an expensive affair. It really involves two arts--itself and music. Then, there is all that needed space where we could put 100 people and teach vertical dance. But we have been through difficult times before, taken risks, found ways to survive, and we will find new and other ways to overcome these limits too. Survival has now become the key word. Survival for this art which has exploded on the campus and the world scene.

There is another kind of survival which cannot help but effect any art and that, of course, is the world we live in. We live in a complex time bombarded with change, where, as Robert Lifton states in History and Human Survival, "Things change over night," "New inventions appear wiping out yesterday's realities," and "We deal with incongruity, disorientation, loss of solid ground." We live in the midst of media bombardment...tearing down of history. It is no wonder, then, that when I asked a student what he hoped to do, he replied, "I just want to be able to live." (We must remember to listen to what students are saying). If art is a way of knowing reality, and it is, how do we help students with _that_ reality? One grabs at a life line--the reminder that art searches, is a way of learning, a way of discipline, a lone and solitary way at the same time wishing, needing to share its findings.

All the explosion is not without its lesser side. Explosion means bursting in all directions from a center. Everywhere shafts of light. Rather like Stephen Leacock's hero who jumped on his horse and rode off madly in all directions. In that dash we have come in danger of losing the human touch. (However abstract...there dances the human creature.) It becomes apparent even in the basics of dance, beginning with technique. Dancers' bodies have greatly improved in the ability to move, but comprehension about the reason for moving has given way to empty ritual or skill for its own sake. Technique must be in the service of performance and choregraphy. We need to close a gap that has sprung up between movement and meaning. We know more about the analysis of movement than we did earlier (and that is good), but we need to teach more about experiencing movement, the way movement feels totally, as well as its analytical aspects. We are overcareful at the expense of experiencing of dancing (the "ings"). Second, lack of interest and involvement in composing have produced mediocre dances, or dances that alienate the audience when performed by technicians who are involved only with their own psychic centers. An understanding of what composing means is needed. These criticisms are not 100% true, but are valid enough to say we must take stock of what and how we are teaching. (Interesting to mention is that outside the campus there are very few teachers of composition.)

Additional pitfalls are elitism, the idea that everyone must become a specialist, and the myth that anyone can teach. We must look for more breadth, but never at the expense of excellence and eloquence.

We need to look at a seemingly contradictory statement, to wit: All dancers should study composition, but not everyone is a choreographer. For understanding and intelligence as a performer, the first half of the statement is true, as process. For the sake of the audience the second half is resoundingly true. Too many dancers with their own companies replete with nothing choreography. This is certainly true of contemporary dance. Ballet has its own parallel in lack of new choreographers, or those who produce pallid works. Consequently, we must be more selective in guiding students and preparing them with the truth about themselves, their strengths, and what they can realistically expect to do in dance. This, in turn, leads to the search for new avenues for dance, new possibilities, and innovations in our thinking.

We need to deepen the human experience and potential of our students in order to enhance the foregoing, and to jealously guard artistic quality in our offerings in the midst of a society which has gone movement berserk (aerobics, dancercise, breaking, flashdance); literature on beauty and exercise (The Body Principle, etc., etc., etc.). I read the same plea for "humanness" in educational and in medical reports. Young interns are strongly advised to nurture and sustain human qualities in their caring for the patient. Can it be that we have discovered the human being? Are we in a new kind of renaissance? A consideration of the individual again--but with other individuals?

Following the human being tack, whatever happened to the audience? While we are teaching art for the sake of the individual's development, talent, growth--as artists, we also want to share. Alienating the audience denies a basic human need to share. I am not suggesting pandering, only, as a well-known critic says, "Let me in on the secret." A young "new waver" says she is ready to stop the alienation act and consider the audience. Good. Otherwise, there flashes across my mind a line from the poetess Stevie Smith, "I'm not waving, I'm drowning."

How will teaching look in the next decade? It might read a little like this:

1. What is the goal?
2. What is the gap between movement and meaning?
3. Seeking human potential.
4. Refinement--making connections amongst all the lines of explosion.
5. Seeking quality and excellence.
6. Musicality.
7. A sense of theatre.
8. Participatory courses for the amateur.

9. Guidance for dance majors.
10. New ideas for student employment.
11. Interdisciplinary courses.
12. Research into movement and rhythm.
13. Training for dance administrators.
14. Research into teaching.

Dorothy Madden
Professor Emeritus
University of Maryland
Founder, Dance Department

*FILM   Film began to appear in university courses during the
1920s. Several schools take credit for offering the "first"
course. Most of these courses were of the "Introduction to
Motion Pictures" type, organized along the broadest lines of
art appreciation with some history and some discussion of
nontechnical techniques. After 50 years, the general introductory course remains today the most widespread of film
courses in the United States, with approximately 800 such
courses offered in almost as many colleges.*

*The first major in film was offered in 1932 by the
University of Southern California, which began a master's
program in cinema in 1935 and established one of the first
Ph.D. programs in film-related work. These USC offerings,
like many today, are in a communications framework. The first
full-fledged scholarly film program with a Ph.D. was established by New York University in 1970.*

*Expansion of film studies did not begin until the postwar
years. The following institutions pioneered the various contexts in which major programs in film were to be offered:*

University	Year film program established	Area
Indiana University	*1944*	*Audio-visual/ Instructional materials*
New York University	*1946*	*Broadcast/Radio-TV*
University of California at Los Angeles	*1947*	*Theater*
Boston University	*1947*	*Communications*

*The following figures indicate the growth of the total number
of film courses (including all courses strongly concerned with
film in any academic context) in the United States from 1946
to 1959:*

Year	Number of Courses
1946	86
1949	113
1953	161
1957	275
1959	305

The major growth in film, however, occurred in the sixties; film in the university is basically a product of this decade. In 1959, only 10 programs around the country offered undergraduate majors in film. In 1971, 47 offered degrees in film, ranging from the A.A. to the Ph.D., with approximately 4,600 undergraduate majors and 1,500 graduate majors in M.A., M.S., M.F.A., and Ph.D. programs. Degrees in cinema, motion pictures, film, and radio-TV-film are now definitely "in." Ninety-six universities without formal film programs in 1971 had students majoring in film, though actually taking their degrees in other subjects. Four hundred and twenty-seven colleges and universities offered more than one course in film. A total of 2,400 courses in film in 1971 compares with 850 courses in 1964.

Between 1916 and 1969, 493 theses and dissertations were presented whose prime subject was film. Of this number, 104 were Ph.D. dissertations, a very large majority of which (at least 70 percent in recent years and 95 percent a decade or more ago) were on the various pedagogic uses of film and often involved statistical research on the effectiveness of instructional films. The first thesis--presented at the University of Iowa in 1916--was on teaching with movies.

Most film programs, even large ones, do not exist as separate administrative entities, but are usually under the jurisdiction of a "large" discipline. If the film curriculum is large, it is usually an area in broadcasting/communications or theater/drama. Over 40 percent of all film curricula in the country are in one or the other of these two administrative units. If a film program is smaller, it may be located anywhere, but the tendency is to locate it in arts/fine arts *departments. About 20 percent of all film programs are in this administrative unit. The next largest area of control is English, which contains about 10 percent of all programs. Independent film departments/schools account for only 5 percent of the national total of film curricula. In short, the "controlling context" for film is seldom film itself, but some other discipline.*

A major characteristic of film curricula is that they tend to be developed in the widest variety of administrative/ academic contexts. In addition to the large areas described above, major film programs are organized within the following disciplines: speech, journalism, instructional media, photography, design, theology/religion, and humanities. Important courses and some programs in film are also found in the areas of political science, foreign language, American studies, engineering, anthropology, social ecology, music, comparative literature, and architecture.

In the past three years, there has been an apparent slowdown in the development of major programs in film. The primary trend during this period has been the appearance of film in the curricula of smaller colleges, particularly those with a "liberal" liberal arts context. Here, the tendency is to open a film course or two in the art department, where the teacher of the film course doubles in other media, primarily photography, mixed media, printmaking, painting, drawing, and design.

Film offerings can be classified into four major categories:

1 Appreciation/history/general/introduction of film and... courses This is historically the oldest category and is today, as it always has been, the most widespread. Most often the courses have unlimited enrollment and serve both as general education courses for all majors and as the beginning of the major sequence for film majors. It is almost always a service course and, as such, the "rent payer," because enrollments are large. The average enrollment in a course of this type (according to data from a survey that includes the spectrum of courses from the largest universities to the smaller colleges) is 200 students. Enrollment in a single course of this kind is, in several instances, up to 500. This large enrollment indicates student interest and reflects the high costs of such a course, for which films must be rented. (Budgets for one course of this type range from $200 to $1,500).

2 *Elementary production, usually with film as a studio art*
This is often the 8mm course. Emphasis is on personal
exploration, on film as a means of personal expression. There
is a wide range of course objectives, but all are nonprofessional. Only the most basic techniques are taught and only
simple equipment is used. In a broadcasting/radio-TV context,
this course would be in 16mm, with emphasis on news and simple
"documentary" shooting. On a number of campuses, this kind
of activity is available only on an extracurricular basis
without credit, though some campuses offer it on both a
curricular and noncurricular basis. In recent years, this
kind of course has shown the most rapid expansion. Enrollment
averages 35 but can go as high as 90.

3 *Professional production* These courses are the core of most
professional programs. They are very expensive to run because
of equipment costs. In some courses, materials (raw stock,
processing) are furnished to students at no extra cost to
them. Some of these subsidies go as high as $500 in advanced
courses. The recent tendency, which is spreading, however, is
to cut back on subsidies by requiring students to pay for
materials. The early practice of organizing the major
curriculum in sharply defined, almost "trade" areas such as
sound recording, editing, etc., is decreasing. Production
courses are becoming broader based, with more emphasis on
developing many skills simultaneously and approaching the
ideal of the "total filmmaker." This is part of a shift in
emphasis away from "job training" for industry and dramatic
films and toward imagist, noncommercial films and films as
documentary. The average production course has 30 students
(graduate or undergraduate) though in a few places enrollments
go up to 60 students.

4 *Scholarly courses* These are advanced courses which deal
with historical aspects of film, theory, and criticism. These
courses, more than those of other categories, conform to the
traditional structuring of college courses. The main emphasis
is on criticism; the secondary concern is review of film
theory. History is also widely reviewed, but there is little
emphasis on researching and writing original history.

In addition to professional production, the teaching of
films as an artistic medium, and/or the scholarly directions
of film work in universities, a major development in the past
two years has been the formation of courses (and full
curricula) for preparing teachers of film for secondary
schools. Over 100 colleges and universities offer courses
especially designed for "film teachers." The number of such

courses has doubled in the past three years.

In 1971, there were approximately 300 full-time and 33 part-time faculty members in departments offering a major in film. Altogether about 1,600 persons teach film in American universities and colleges, with a greater prevalence of part-time teachers than in many other academic areas. Over 50 percent of the people teaching film full time have no "film degree," but majored in some other subject. This is particularly true of people who have been teaching for the past 10 years, with the film degree holder almost nonexistent among senior faculty--as is typical of the early developmental stage of any emerging academic discipline. There is presently a heavily accelerated "Ph.D.-ization" of film teaching. This move includes the production area, where there is an increasing number of teachers from academically oriented programs rather than from "studio" arts. Thus, a small segment of people who teach production never practiced, but only studied it.

The major professional organizations are (1) the University Film Association, founded in 1947, with approximately 350 members, over half of whom are not teaching but work in film production on the campus, making sponsored educational films; and (2) the Society for Cinema Studies, founded in 1959. This is the major scholarly society for film with a membership of approximately 120. Membership is open by invitation only and candidacy is reviewed and voted on by members. The College Art Association, the American Theatre Association, and the Speech Association of America have component parts concerned with film or have at one time or another expressed interest in problems of film teaching.

Several resource organizations exist. The American Film Institute, founded in 1967, acts as a clearinghouse in certain film education activities, runs special shows in Washington D.C., theaters, and is trying to work with film archives. It is active in cataloging and publishing basic reference works in film and also runs a "training and research center" on the West Coast for 40 young people with either film making or scholarly film interests. This program is roughly equal in standards to most of the major graduate film programs in American universities but is perhaps more closely tied with the Hollywood film industry. The American Federation of Film Societies has a membership of about 500, which is approximately one-eighth of the total number of film societies in the United States, most of which are college-related. These societies provide key showings of important films for their respective campuses. Almost every United States campus has one or more film series or society, and frequently these groups serve as beachheads for the formal introduction of film into the curriculum. The major film archives are at the Library of Congress in Washington D.C., the Museum of Modern Art in New York City, and the George Eastman House in Rochester, New York. Their respective holdings are extensive, but even collectively neither their efforts nor their resources are equivalent to peer groups in other countries.

Resources and the costs thereof are a major problem in film. In scholarly areas, films themselves are the prime resource material. But prints are expensive, and no college library can acquire them the way they acquire books, not only because of the expense but also because of copyright problems and the unavailability of prints. More prints of more films for more showings over longer lending periods for vastly cheaper rates are greatly needed. Many schools with film programs do have extensive book collections. A "good" collection of books on film numbers about 1,000 volumes. Basic older works have been reprinted extensively.

Costs of equipment and materials for production courses are also high. The average cost of a film thesis for an M.F.A. is about $900.

The recent "leveling" in university income and enrollments could lead to some setbacks for film, which is still a somewhat suspect subject in many college curricula. Film is especially vulnerable because of (1) the high costs of its programs, (2) its recent establishment in most cases (universities may operate on a last-in, first-out basis), and (3) questions of academic tradition and justification.

As far as the discipline itself is concerned, there is a need for clarification of student interests and societal possibilities in the different areas within the subject and a need for a better understanding of what kind of balance between the following is possible and desirable:

1 Film as part of general education Here elementary experience in film making and moderate investigation of the academic aspects of film are provided in a context in which production courses are parallels of basic creative writing courses, even of basic "expression" courses such as English Composition. Emphasis is on communication, reaching out, expression, with film serving as an alternative or additional means to create, inform, show, and feel. There is also concern for "appreciation"--getting to know more about film.

2 Film as yet another medium available to the studio artist who senses the limitations of one medium breaking down and requires skills and experience in order to expand his total range of art tools. This trend involves film in all kinds of mixed media developments and events.

3 Film as a major subject for professionally oriented students Here there are points of tension between acquiring skills and training for existing job descriptions in the "industry" and acquiring skills needed for following a more personal vision. What kind of balance should there be between a background of skills and a body of personal work? Also, should the old nineteenth-century, but still overwhelming, idea of art as intimate, personal, internalized, individual creation be de-emphasized in favor of work that attempts more directly to reach out?

4 Film as a subject of scholarly concern Scholarly work is being done in film by students and established scholars, but is still uneven in both cases. Comparative studies, particularly those related to literary concerns, are dominant. Film historiography is very poor. There is yet no fully adequate general textbook of film history, and even specialized works on film history are weak. Structural analysis is rising as a critical method and seems promising.

Film cannot escape connections with other arts--and with other cultures. Some new definition of medium is needed, as film is often too sharply defined. Perhaps, as with other established media, film needs to be looked at not as a total profession, trade, subject, discipline, or medium--not as a thing complete in itself with its own rules--but rather as one of many possible means to work with moving pictures.

Notes

Note: This section on film is based on an unpublished manuscript by Joseph Anderson (1972), director of the film program at Ohio University.

FILM
(Updated)

Training in film and television education in the university
certainly has changed in the last ten years. Three obvious
pressure areas are:

Technological growth Here, we are talking about both
quantitative and qualitative changes in technology. We
have advances ranging from disks, tapes, satellite
optical fiber transmission, use of cybernetics of one
kind or another, to the whole array of forces that
substantially impact the way film and television is
produced and must be taught.

Economic change There is now a plurality of outlets
ranging from pay TV to cable, to theatrical and non-
theatrical distribution, plus the creation of a whole new
market in audiovisual publishing, which entails training
in production and distribution.

Social pressure Possibly the major item on our domestic
social agenda in the next ten years will be, who owns the
airways, and who should have access to them. The political element in the question of control will loom large as
we enter a revolutionary period in the media.

Naturally, all of this growth is reflected onto film/televi-
sion education and some big changes will or must be taking
place.

Certainly, that impact will occur at a general level of
education. The question of audiovisual literacy both at the
level of reading materials, as well as the actual level of
production, will become integrated into the school system in
the very earliest grades and will become increasingly
important.

Here, we are concerned only with training at the university level and the ways in which technological change, economic infrastructures, and social pressures will impact teaching
and research at the highest professional plateau.

The field of film/television studies is two-dimensional.
On one side is production--on the other, criticism. But no
longer can these people be viewed in "splendid isolation."
Virtually every department on campus will become involved and

interaction will intensify. For example, people view our film materials not because they are interested in the production of film for television, not even because they are interested in the history of film and television, but because they see this as a primary documentation on our popular culture, answering ecological questions, and departments such as history and sociology now have deep and abiding concern with film education.

Motion picture and television departments were once classically distinct disciplines. Increasingly, there is more and more overlap and curriculum crossover. Someone trained in film making must also be trained in the handling of video equipment for wider, more aesthetic possibilities. Department overlap will continue to expand in all teaching areas that benefit from interactive systems of one kind or another.

Bob Rosen
Theater Arts, Motion Picture
Television
University of California, Los
Angeles

CREATIVE OR POETIC WRITING   Writing has always been part of instruction in English, whether it meant teaching the skills of expository prose or encouraging students to express their own imaginings. Special classes gradually evolved in various schools in which the prime focus was on making works of art with words. Often these classes have been called <u>creative writing</u> courses, though perhaps this term does not ade<u>quately</u> capture the distinctive spirit of the endeavor; when a biologist writes up the results of his research, for example, his writing may be new and creative. Perhaps "poetic writing" better expresses the artistic connotations involved in making something new with words alone, though in this case novels, short stories, and graffiti, as well as poetry, would be considered poetic. At any rate, there is a growing awareness on the campus that creative writing is as much an art as sculpture or dance.

Only recently has there been a movement to identify university writing programs with the other arts. In 1967, Charles D. Wright of the University of North Carolina was the first li<u>terary</u> artist ever invited to speak to a conference of the Natio<u>nal</u> Council of the Arts in Education. In addition, only recently have there been efforts to identify creative writing programs within the offerings of English departments and to form a national professional association of these programs. An organization called Associated Writing Programs was established in the last half of the sixties and now has between 50 and 60 affiliated member institutions. The following are the objectives of this association, as expressed by its founder, novelist R.V. Cassill of Brown University (cited in Wright, 1967, p. 38):

1 To set up a clearinghouse (or agency) to place writers more usefully and profitably in the mainstream of literary education...

2 To build a new publishing and reading community within the academic community, among the academic multitudes...

3 To support and define the M.F.A. as a terminal degree for those whose primary and long-term commitment to letters is a commitment to writing and its relevant disciplines.

Originally, the association affiliated only institutions with some type of graduate program in creative writing, but in 1971 it began to accept members with only undergraduate work, including community colleges.

In 1968, the College English Association, with the cooperation of the Book-of-the-Month Club, published for the first time a <u>Directory of Creative Writing Programs in the United States and Canada</u>. This directory and the second edition, which was published in 1970, provide listings of creative writing programs that are within English departments in four-year institutions. (Expository and technical writing courses are excluded). In 1968, there were 680 such programs with 491 full-time and 920 part-time faculty members. In 1970, there were 817 programs with 543 full-time and 1,245 part-time faculty members. In 1970, 27 institutions sponsored or hosted writers' conferences and summer workshops. Thirty-seven institutions offered an undergraduate major or concentration in creative writing, fifty-eight offered graduate programs in creative writing or a creative M.A. thesis option, and four offered Ph.D. programs. Two hundred and forty-two schools had a writer-in-residence of some type. well-established programs, to name only a few, exist at the University of Iowa, San Francisco State, Johns Hopkins, Indiana University, Boston University, the University of Oregon, and the University of North Carolina at Greensboro.

Needless to say, there are many additional creative writing courses in two-year colleges and also outside English departments. Sometimes, though rarely, writing is part of an interdisciplinary fine arts program. Sometimes it is an elective within a school of journalism. Sometimes it is in a department of radio, TV, and film or in a theater department. The dimensions of these offerings are as yet unknown.

The appearance of creative writing in a variety of areas points out, however, the obvious fact that writing is deeply related to many of the other arts. In his 1967 address to the Conference on the Arts in Education, Charles Wright (1967, p. 42) said, "I think a creative writing program is most likely to flourish when it is part of a large and varied involvement in the arts on a campus...Though it is hard to measure, there is a kind of symbiosis by which creative writing thrives on a campus."

Notes

Note: When the Institute of American Indian Arts was created at Santa Fe, New Mexico, eight years ago, the Indian staff simply installed creative writing as one of the arts without much ado.

CREATIVE WRITING
(Updated)

I am often undecided whether to boast of being the product of an international formal education experienced on three continents or to complain of being the victim of a much scattered and broken schooling. But as either product or victim, I think I should begin by pointing out that, at least in my experience, it is only in American colleges and universities that "creative writing," or, as Jack has preferred to call it in his original survey, "poetic writing," is considered in any way to be a valid academic subject.

In the Chinese kindergarten of my youth and during my sporadic education in Chinese following that exciting year, one learned at least an adequate calligraphy and vocabulary, which meant that one could put together an acceptably traditional essay or standard set of verses. More than that, one could produce a perfectly predictable, but still decorative, scroll of bamboo shoots and leaves for the summer, peach blossoms on a black bough for spring, chrysanthemums for autumn, and a correct winter snow scene. None of these qualified one to be called either a writer or an artist--they were simply standard equipment.

In the Oxford of my day, one was expected to enter already able to produce adequate expository prose. As an undergraduate your tutor might require an essay a week on which to vent his aggressions and spleen, but by the time one was admitted to advanced work one was presumably able to teach oneself whatever one needed to learn, and with a minimum of guidance.

It was only in my college years in America that I was able to get academic credit for writing short stories and producing verse. As a result of this I have always carried a burden of guilt--a very modest and bearable one, I admit--but I think it is the kind of guilt that Thomas Mann once wrote of in saying that he had always felt himself akin to the criminal by actually earning a better than average living through cheating the respectable worlds of commerce and wage-earning by fabricating fictions.

I risk this personal note because I hold quite mixed and contradictory views on many of the issues involved. I am frequently of three minds. I remember that during the activist '60s my children used to consult me, with generous condescension, from time to time on what I thought about various issues disturbing or stimulating the colleges and universities they were attending. At one point, one of them said, "You always sound so sympathetic with a lot of what's going on, but at the same time you're terribly stuffy about its academic importance." I recall trying to answer by saying, "Well, it seems to me that all-night nude parties with a supply of liquor and pot have always been a healthy part of the educational experience, but I'm not sure that they deserve the awarding of grade-points."

My impression of the situation today, and I suspect it will obtain during the rest of the 80s and into the 90s is that the purely academic recognition of "creative" or "poetic" writing had reached a peak, or even crested, a decade ago.

The usefulness of an M.F.A. or a Ph.D. in creative writing has lessened simply because it has ceased to be as marketable as it once was.

On the other hand, I would say that today all major universities and most 4-year liberal arts colleges not only provide adequate instruction, either through courses or individual contracts, in the elements of writing verse and fiction. They also provide a living for a number of writers and poets of rank who prefer the academy to the worlds of journalism or publishing. And almost all of these writers are approachable and generous. This is perhaps the most important aspect for the student writer--to be able to meet and speak on a one-to-one basis with a published and publishing writer who is willing to take the time to read his work and discuss it frankly.

It is hardly an original observation that the American university performs many functions not considered elsewhere as strictly academic. That is one of its most enlivening, as well as demanding and baffling, qualities; for at some point one must decide just where the university's role should end. Though qualified as a scholar to handle the utility as well as some specialized courses in the gamut of English and American literature, I was actually hired by the Department of English here as a writer, and I treasure my letter of appointment, which reads in part, "The publishing that (he) is now achieving in magazines such as Harper's and The New Yorker, and his books printed by Knopf, are to be considered the equivalent of scholarly publications by his colleagues in the learned journals and will carry equal weight in consideration of his advancement through the regular ranks of the professorship." And that from a department famed at the time for its belief in historical scholarship and criticism as the one true faith.

In a recent work, Making College Pay Off, by Adele Scheele, a number of writers, TV producers, directors, and such pay tribute to this function of the American university. I don't know what instructors in playwriting or screenwriting or musical composition experience, but at least in English the instructor in verse and fiction soon discovers that he is expected to be the poor students psychiatrist and intimate adviser.

In this sense, the American university has become even more involved than it was ten years ago in the rather difficult sphere to define or limit. After all, the one true end of this kind of instruction is to enable the young and original writer to achieve publication. Not simply student publication, which is relatively easy and is nevertheless significant, but publication for a larger audience. And here one finds a variety of responses from the academic community. The commercial publishing world itself has become more and more monolithic, dominated by conglomerates. The most recent piece of popular fiction of which I am part-author is the publication of a formerly independent house now part of the Putnam Group, which in turn is owned by Universal, itself the property of MCA, and if MCA is not God it at least owns a large section of His stock.

Many writers have themselves begun to deal with this situation by founding their own small presses, and the journal Small Press appears six times a year. This is not vanity publishing, though some of these presses are primarily interested in fine printing. Certain university presses have supported the publication of original poetry over the years. Yale's series of young poets is well known and important. Wesleyan and Indiana have recently published a number of titles, as has Minnesota. But for the greater part, the university presses publish poetry only in translation or collected editions of the dead. Everyone knows that collections of verse and short stories are the least saleable of literary works. It is interesting to note that a few years ago, a group of university presses banded together to publish once a year, and in rotation, a collection of short fiction given the Drue Heinz Literature Prize. The most recent (and third) winner has just been announced by the University of Pittsburgh Press, Jonathan Penner's Private Parties. One collection of short stories a year seems very little, but it may be the cloud the size of a man's hand.

Another involvement, and an increasingly important one, is the support by various colleges and universities of writers conferences. A recent issue of Publishers Weekly deals with four on the coast, two of which are supported by local institutions, the University of California, San Diego and Loyola Marymount University in Los Angeles.

It is perhaps in these directions that one should look for the campus's increasing involvement in creativity in writing.

John Espey
Professor Emeritus
English Department
University of California,
Los Angeles

MUSIC   *Beginning in the Middle Ages, the stewardship, support, and thrust for the dissemination and influence of music gradually shifted from the church to the aristocracy. In the last century, the conservatory briefly but intensely took over these functions, and today they have been assumed, for the greater part, by the universities.*

Music was, of course, one subject of the quadrivium, and by the end of the Middle Ages it had been assigned a singular place in the curricula of some Western universities. The Oxford statutes of 1431 give such an indication. Cambridge granted a bachelor of music degree as early as 1463, Oxford as early as 1499.

Limited evidence exists of music study in American institutions of education in the first 100 years of their existence. That music was a part of college study at Harvard is implied in a tract written by a graduate of 1698.

The musical societies, singing societies, and musical clubs of communal life migrated to the campuses during the latter part of the eighteenth century. By 1800, performing organizations were sufficiently numerous for one to conclude that they were a normal, expected part of college life. Records of significant university events, principally commencement programs, provide evidence of such groups at the University of Pennsylvania, Harvard, Yale, Dartmouth, et al. Enigmatically, music, which was firmly implanted at Oxford as a part of academe with a faculty of its own by the end of the Middle Ages, did not develop in the United States as an appropriate instructional subject in higher education until the latter part of the nineteenth century.

The earliest instruction in music at the normal school, college, and university in this country was in vocal music. This early training, which appeared first in normal schools, served the purpose of preparing students to teach music, but the emphasis was on music as a cultural study. From about 1835 to 1870, as music appeared at the collegiate level, efforts were consistently directed toward making music an integral part of the curriculum by convincing students and administrations of the instructional values of music.

In 1835, one year after vocal music was officially introduced into the Boston public schools, the normal school at Lexington, Massachusetts, provided opportunities for vocal music study. Within the next 10 years, offerings in music appeared at three other normal schools in the Northeast--at

Westfield, Massachusetts; Bridgewater, Massachusetts; and Albany, New York. By 1835, Oberlin College had a professor of sacred music and 30 years later the conservatory was established. Harvard was offering lectures in music by 1862, but not until 1870 were courses offered on a regular basis (i.e., providing credit for degree programs). In that year, a course in the history of music and elective courses in harmony and counterpoint were available. Vassar College provided music courses as early as 1867, and by 1872 eight of its forty-two instructors were teaching music.

Concomitantly, conservatories developed rapidly and abundantly. The movement began with the establishment of a conservatory at East Greenwich, Rhode Island, in 1859 and one in Providence a little later. The Oberlin Conservatory, as mentioned, was founded in 1865. The New England Conservatory, organized in 1867, was incorporated in 1870. The year 1867 was a rich one for the development of musical culture in the United States. Founded in that year, along with the New England Conservatory, were the Boston Conservatory, the Chicago Musical College, and the Cincinnati Conservatory. Within the following 20 years, other outstanding conservatories were formed, including the Dana Musical Institute, the Detroit Conservatory, the College of Music of Cincinnati, the New York College of Music, the Cleveland Conservatory, and the American Conservatory of Chicago. Several of these schools still provide the musical world with some of its most respected professional musicians.

By 1915, music as an academic discipline had been accepted by colleges and universities across the United States. Departments, schools, and colleges of music had evolved into established units within private and public institutions of higher education. All state universities with any degree of sophistication had such units. Music as culture and method had blossomed lavishly on campuses; from extracurricular activities of vocal and instrumental performance, music grew to full recognition at the collegiate level for the development of the performer, historian, and educator.

During the upsurge of collegiate departments of music and conservatories, many independent schools appeared under the title "conservatory." Some truly deserved the distinction of the title, but many were one-room, one-person entities totally unworthy of such distinction. The same conditions prevailed in varying degrees on campuses. Fortunately, the Depression of the thirties took a heavy toll among these conservatories of lesser standards. Unfortunately, the Depression led to the bankruptcy of some conservatories which were contributing significantly to musical culture. Depressed conditions, along with spiraling operational costs in the 1940s, closed virtually all remaining major conservatories except the most financially stalwart and those allied with institutions of higher education.

The disparate quality of music offerings and the disparate content of curricula in both conservatories and departments of music had led in 1927 to the formation of a national accrediting agency, the National Association of Schools of Music (NASM). As a result of the work of NASM, definable standards exist and, although curricula and degrees vary, a national norm had developed.

Accredited Institutions of Higher Education, 1971-72, published for the Federation of Regional Accrediting Commissions of Higher Education by the American Council on Education, lists 1,999 accredited universities, colleges, and junior colleges. An estimated 1,500 have music in some form. NASM's Music in Higher Education, 1970-71, a summary of information from the annual reports of member institutions, indicates enrollments of 45,333 undergraduate music majors, 6,167 master's level students, and 1,724 doctoral candidates. The summary indicates that these data represent reports of 287 member institutions from a total of 385. During the same reporting period Students Enrolled for Advanced Degrees, issued by the Office of Education of the U.S. Department of Health, Education and Welfare, indicated that 8,471 students were enrolled for advanced degrees in 884 reporting institutions. The Directory of Music Faculties in Colleges and Universities, U.S. and Canada, 1970-72 lists 14,500 faculty members (362 of whom teach in Canada) in 1,300 different colleges, universities, conservatories, schools of music, and community colleges.

Notes

Note: This section on music is based on an unpublished manuscript by Frank S. Stillings (1972), dean of the School of Fine and Applied Arts at Central Michigan University.

MUSIC
(Updated)

The flourishing university of the future will be the university that offers special training or fulfills a specific need that cannot be duplicated elsewhere at less cost. Fierce competition from state schools is going to force the private institution to demonstrate and substantiate its reason for existence. Public support will be a major factor sustaining the private school. Two popular windows through which the public views the university are the athletic programs and the college of fine and performing arts. All too often, quick opinions are formed from a superficial analysis of what is seen. Each university competes for public attention and support through its athletic program. It participates according to its convictions and according to its funds. Unfortunately, overall success of the university is often erroneously measured by the public as a simple win/lose tally of their athletic efforts. The frequently neglected college of fine arts is a powerful instrument; building a positive image for the university when properly employed. The public responds when the programs of the university are timely, appropriate, and significant. The university that projects the finest image is the university that will receive the most financial support, build the best faculty and attract the most talented students.

The college of fine arts, generally, does not approach the education of its students with the fervor or make the demands upon its students that are made by the other colleges of the university. I find the degree requirements in basic skills at the undergraduate level to be far below the level demanded from young artists when they begin their careers. In my own field, I have rarely, if ever, found a graduate adequately prepared in basic skills to meet the challenge of a performance career in the arts. The nurturing and refining of the young singer is, at best, a personal and individual effort. Even if the student possesses a world class vocal gift, the accompanying skills needed are in disarray at graduation.

Most fine arts programs are performance oriented. I believe the major thrust of a training program should be teaching the student how to prepare material for performance, rather than emphasizing the performances. Music students are often graduated without really being taught the technique of preparing music for performance.

The talented fine arts student has easy access to the artistic life of the area. This is especially true of music students, in general, and of singers in particular. Singers are self-contained performance units. They have a unique ability to show their wares instantaneously. There is no barrier between the singer and the audience. There is an ongoing overall fascination with the gifted singer. Painters, sculptors, and other graphic artists are more or less detached from their work. Actors, conductors and stage directors need elaborate trappings and long preparation to show their talents. Even the pianist is sometimes limited by the quality of the instrument supplied. The impact of the talented singer is personal and immediate. They move quickly into the area's music and theatre circles: the church choir, the civic chorus and the amateur/professional theatre and opera groups. They also have easy access to the business community through performances for local civic and service clubs. A community of talented, accomplished singers, because of their high visibility, will make a major contribution to the positive image of the university and will help attract talented students to all fine arts programs.

Singing is an emotional and intellectual communication. The emotional aspect of the communication is supplied by temperament, gift, talent or some other indefinable factor coming from deep within the performer. The ability to communicate emotionally, generally, cannot be taught; however, it can be nurtured and refined. Intellectual communication, on the other hand, offers a wide area of teachable skills. Memorization technique, intellectual concept, historical understanding, exact translation and the position/function of the character within the confines of the drama should stand in the forefront of the program of instruction. Equal efforts should be made in the area of performance skills, i.e., audition technique, acting, dancing and physical conditioning. Each student should be actively engaged in an extensive investigation of song literature and in the building of standard operatic repertory. A large number of standard roles, well within the grasp of the student, should be thoroughly studied musically, dramatically, and linguistically. In effect, the student should be stockpiling roles for future use. Most academic programs overlook the value of this study. It is mandatory for the career-minded student.

It is most unusual for the aspiring American singer to achieve adequate foreign language training while pursuing an undergraduate degree. Sight singing and keyboard skills are generally below minimum standards. Young singers are welcomed into professional ranks when they are masters of these skills. It is generally the practice of the conductor to select the better musician rather than the better voice, if there is a choice. This is particularly true if the singer is unknown.

The American singer is often excluded from the inner circle of the European conductor and stage director because of language deficiency. It is necessary for the young opera singer to master a conversational ability in both German and Italian. Even more to the point, the singer's language ability must be facile enough to release them to concentrate on the meaning of the text at the moment of performance. Without this ability, a convincing performance in a foreign language is nearly impossible.

I believe it is the responsibility of the university to supply the student with an opportunity to learn these skills. In my experience, I have found these skills missing much of the time. The opera companies of the United States routinely fill their rosters with young Italian and German singers who sometimes possess vocal abilities inferior to their American counterparts. This situation is generally attributable to the American short fall in language ability. If American singers are to continue to achieve in the realm of international music, these voids must be filled, both linguistically and musically.

The aspiring opera singer must be well versed in the interrelation of the arts. A comprehensive course correlating the history and development of literature, drama, art and music is an essential study for all arts students.

The philosophy of business, its principles and procedures, is an area totally ignored by most arts programs. It is of the utmost importance that the career-minded student be thoroughly schooled in the techniques of salesmanship and negotiation. Business courses for the student artist must also include a foundation in finance, bookkeeping, and the fundamentals of advertising. This study is crucial for the professional artist.

The time is right for an assertive university to move into the area of professional training and assume a commanding position. In music, this can be done, I believe, by stimulating the program from the top. There are many graduates prowling the corridors of professional music looking for a way to enter. The university could attract the most talented of these people by implementing a graduate level program that actually recruits gifted graduates, brings them to the campus and supplies them with a concerted opportunity to refine the skills necessary for a major career.

Many of the essentials of this program are already in place at a major university. The existing music, language, history and business departments should be utilized. Minor adjustments could be made to fill certain areas pertinent only to the arts students.

The cost of establishing and maintaining a professional training program is disproportionate to its many benefits for the student and for the university. With proper implementation and administration, some of its graduates will achieve their goals and succeed at the highest professional level, and the university will enjoy the attendant reflection.

William Walker
Baritone
Metropolitan Opera, NYC
1962-1980

VISUAL ARTS   It is clearly true that the visual arts have moved onto the academic stage with no intention of leaving it (College Art Association of America, 1966). In spite of the evident excellence of many independent professional art schools, the idea of college is firmly implanted in the minds of many as the culminating reach of the educational process for artists. We do not, as in Germany, the Scandinavian countries, and other European nations, parallel university education with technical and crafts schools having equal (and substantial) state support. Our efforts instead reflect our individualistic attitudes toward education in the arts and echo our notions of free enterprise and variety in education generally. The first formal commitment to the education of artists (at institutional levels, as distinguished from goodness knows how many apprenticeship arrangements) was the school established as the Pennsylvania Academy of the Fine Arts in 1806. This school is still with us, still offering studio work without dependence on the degree credential our society weighs so heavily. Other schools followed: Maryland Institute (1826), the School of the Art Institute of Chicago, which preceded the museum (1866), Massachusetts College of Arts (1873), the School of the Boston Museum of Fine Arts (1876), Cleveland Institute (1882), Kansas City Art Institute (1885), Minneapolis Art Institute (1886), Corcoran School of Art (1887), Brooklyn Museum Art School (1898), and John Herron School of Art (1902). All these were functioning early as studio centers for preparing painters and sculptors. But George Fisk Comfort at Syracuse in 1873 and John Ferguson Weir at Yale in 1869, along with the founders of art programs at the University of Illinois (1876) and a few other places, conceived practice in the arts as having humanistic values that were compatible with other, more literary, university pursuits. The invasion of the colleges by artists was an inevitable consequence, and art programs proliferated after 1900.

There was, in the beginning, no problem of separating the intentions of the independent professional schools from those of the colleges. The independent schools were looser in administrative organization and more flexible in their acceptance of students than the colleges could be. They were also less likely to infringe on the autonomy of studio professors. They remained indifferent to grades, credits, or final accolades. They were, in short, cast in the European atelier mold. The colleges, on the other hand, could not exempt a large class of students--art students--from the limitations imposed on the rest. They began to develop curricula that involved choices of activities and combinations

*of faculty members to match. Their scheduling and require-
ments formed an intricate network through which the student
moved in accord with prevailing academic routines. Faculty
members in the arts, in contrast with the part-time independent schoolteachers, reached for and gained all the rights,
privileges, and perquisites (including tenure and committee
assignments) of their fellow faculty members on campus. Artists in some numbers rejected the idea of regular employment
as an erosion of their freedom to create in their own imagery.
Others found the processes of eating regularly, working under
institutional roofs, raising families with comparative security, and even, in a few places, occupying studios rent free a
not too stultifying experience. The universities and colleges
probably scrutinized the teaching capacities (though not
necessarily the academic credentials) of an artist more closely than did their independent counterparts. Generally speaking, docile types tended to move toward the college studios,
both as teachers and as students. More adventurous spirits,
or those who could not for long tolerate any kind of prescrip-
tion, continued to use the looser, more permissive, independent professional schools to gain whatever advantages they
could from teachers with some reputation as artists and from
association with free spirits of their own kind in an environment often enhanced (in the museum schools) by rich collections open for study and ready for exploitation by teachers
and students alike.*

*In the 1930s, a curious trend began. As a result of
pressures developing in state departments of education aimed
at making teacher certification requirements more rigorous,
independent schools like the School of the Art Institute of
Chicago, which had long had respectable teacher education
programs in art, were nudged toward "improvement" of their
credentials. Though credit from an unsanctioned professional
school might have status among administrators locally, it
could be rejected by school officials in the next state, for
there was no "accredited" list of these schools. Professional
art schools began the difficult process of moving into the
charmed circle of the accredited schools (the colleges)
through sporadic efforts to qualify for membership in the
regional associations and thus gain inclusion on an acceptable
"list." In Chicago, it took two years of preparation and two
reviews before the Art Institute's effort succeeded. The
North Central Association did not admit another art school for
20 years at least. The Art Institute's pattern of development
in its degree programs involved the addition of general
humanities studies to its studio and art history core. These
"academic" courses could be taken in any accredited schools,*

though most students found it convenient to use the University of Chicago's downtown college, which offered a generous range of late afternoon and evening classes. The B.F.A. was established as a respectable degree in this independent art school, and perhaps in others, to the benefit of teachers, state scholarship recipients, returning veterans with government educational benefits, rehabilitation students, and many more. Parents (who as a class tended to regard arts education with mistrust) were softened at the sight of a degree program in an art institute prospectus and overlooked the skylighted unorthodoxy of the cindery studios strung along the Illinois Central tracks.

To dwell on this transition from purely studio-centered instruction to a mixture of studio and general studies is only a way of emphasizing how effective the mixture became, how potent the combination of studio and classroom was, and of noting the relative promptness of colleges to develop the opportunity they now had within their reach. College-based programs in studio arts grew slowly before World War II but, nourished by the flow of returning veterans, they grew rapidly after the war both in numbers and in academic importance. The colleges, indifferent, unaware, or believing the arts to be polite and amenable pursuits, patted the camel's nose as it appeared inside the tent.

It has been suggested that there are other, more appropriate, ligatures between the practice of art and the traditional academic disciplines than the incorporation of studio courses into the family of campus curricula. Generally, such speculations go back to something like the art institute pattern, but with degree-granting authority moving toward the college partner and practice assigned as the proper responsibility of a satellite institute or conservatory. Such a division of labor obviously preserves the sanctity of scholarship while allowing students to study the things they really want to learn. There was perhaps once a moment in history when such institutional arrangements could have become the rule rather than the exception. It appears to be far too late now to go into reverse on any very general scale. Practicing artists have found their way into the patterns of academe without (as they have discovered) losing their identity as professionals. They are firmly installed on faculties. The visual arts they teach have accommodated themselves on the campus to the mechanical problems of scheduling, grades, and credits that go along with college membership.

In the process of being assimilated, studio faculties have forfeited in many cases their privilege of accepting and retaining for studio instruction only students who show initial dedication and continuing ability to perform well as independent problem solvers. Among the compromises confronting studio teachers is trying to come to terms with nonprofessional students—those who use art as a means of satisfying curiosity, as recreational release, or as a balance to heavy academic fare. In many cases, the resulting programs have yielded excellent creative and educational fruit. The humanities have embraced the arts as brothers—or at least cousins; the arts have become naturalized even when they are not fully integrated. The parallel phenomenon is worth noting. As art has gained in academic respectability, as graduates have moved out of the colleges into the academic marketplace, the degree syndrome has influenced administrative judgments. Art faculty members are not quite the free agents they once were; the degree credential, having become more common, has been confused with artistic or teaching competence. It is a case of the colleges succumbing to their own propaganda: students have been guided toward degree programs; have moved toward intellectualization; and art generally has produced a new generation of idea-oriented artists, capable of thinking art-as-object right out of existence. All this may have been inevitable in any case. But the independent or studio-based professional schools have responded to the challenge of campus-based artist-teachers by themselves moving toward the colleges in both intention and process.

The American Art Directory of the American Federation of Arts (1970) provides information on the scope and dimensions of art programs in the United States today. This directory lists professional art schools, colleges, and universities that offer a major in art; schools of architecture; and individual artists who conduct classes of professional standards. Data, including number of full-time and part-time faculty, degrees offered, majors enrolled, tuition costs, etc., are given for each listing. An extract from this list of college and university programs in the visual arts indicates 605 four-year institutions and 74 two-year institutions, or a total of 679 schools offering a major in art. (Schools of architecture are not included in these extracted numbers). Full-time faculty number 7,275 in four-year schools and 433 in two-year schools, a total of 7,708. Part-time faculty number 2,934 in four-year schools and 185 in two-year schools, a total of 3,119. This is a total faculty of 10,827. Not all schools reported the number of majors enrolled, but 57,100 in four-

year institutions and 4,855 in two-year institutions, or a total of 61,955, were indicated (see note 9). In addition to these numbers are the schools (often schools of museums) that offer courses in joint programs with a partner university, which is the degree-granting institution. Examples of this arrangement are the Corcoran School of Art/George Washington University and the Art Academy of Cincinnati/University of Cincinnati.

What the future holds is not easy to foresee. Art will survive, through the forms it takes, both as an educational enterprise and as each art in its own idiosyncratic development. These changes, perhaps radical, will be conditioned by the emergence of new social, technological, philosophical, and human opportunities. A good part of the changes will reflect the residual effect of art as a college-based educational enterprise. The colleges have the obligation as well as the opportunity to make the process work.

Notes

Note: This section on visual arts is based on an unpublished manuscript by Norman L. Rice (1972), dean of the College of Fine Arts at Carnegie-Mellon University.

9 Information on class enrollments of "students majoring in art and of others taking art courses" is provided, but the data are essentially impossible to interpret since some schools are obviously reporting their entire college enrollment without so indicating and others may be doing this also. In addition, it is not specified that these figures are for an academic year.

VISUAL ARTS
(Updated)

In looking ahead to teaching fine arts in future decades, there are two areas or phases of art education that must be addressed. Both those educational segments are of utmost importance and are, of a certainty, organically related.

Many institutions offer an introductory or foundation program which furnishes the building materials for the creative life ahead. These programs root themselves in the essential investigation of sound drawing and painting technique. It would be tragic to temper or weaken such programs in the future or attempt to find quick and easy paths through them, or to discard them altogether. To be sure, such programs are, for the most part, conservative, speaking of established and workable truths and are necessarily observant of the past.

As I reflect upon my own student years at the Pennsylvania Academy, what impressed me most was not the wit, wisdom, or reputation of the faculty, but its essential belief in the principle of continuity, the sense of a stimulating present made possible by the great traditions of the past. No short cuts were encouraged, and the students' education was built in a series of orderly and well-disciplined steps.

The young student knocking on the door of Brancusi's studio, holding a Brancusi-inspired work for which he expected approbation, received the response he deserved from the master. He was told to go back and start at the proper point of departure, the beginning.

In borrowing Albert Ryder's effective metaphor of the worm, hovering at the end of the branch, reaching out into the untried, the creative unknown, it would seem that any successful art program in the future must forsake neither the branch which makes the first part of the journey possible, nor the beckoning and often forbidding space beyond, which is the true point of departure of creative expression. The second part of the journey is made possible because of all the months and years of preparation.

It is in this second, more subjective phase of the student's art educational experience that the teacher has the greatest opportunity to make use of innovation and flexibility. Here the student is encouraged to look in more

personal directions and to begin coming to grips with some of
the more difficult problems and questions. A reliance upon
system and the past is slowly replaced with a more subjective
response to subject and experience. The student begins the
task of "finding himself" in relation to his aims and
materials.

This is the most difficult, challenging and enjoyable
phase of teaching, simply because here there are few formulas.
I offer the line from Lao Tzu on this occasion when he defines
the ideal teacher as someone "who guides without interfering."
The teacher helps to show the way but gives the student ample
space in which to succeed or fail.

As we look ahead to an ever increasing interest in the
arts in American colleges and universities and with all of our
headlong rushing into the future, it seems more imperative
than ever that we not forget what has been both sane and
workable in the past. Newness means little in and of itself,
and total dedication to change can be self-destructive.

It is tempting to be seduced by the new technologies.
Certainly many of the advanced materials should be considered
and used and may, indeed, replace some of the old. With all
the twenty-year-ago predictions of panaceas, I am still
heartened to see most of my students painting with oil paint
on canvas. The old problems and methods still pertain.

We can most certainly look forward to and have already
been experiencing an accelerated process in art education,
much of which has been beneficial. By increased access to
slides and exhibitions and avenues of easier approach to the
sources of our culture, it is now possible for the student to
go further in any program than ever before. I am always happy
to find students in advance of faculty at a given age. At the
same time, we must not rush our students into professionalism,
but rather allow them ample time to be students.

Our growing knowledge of and involvement in "one world"
can only be a benefit to all. How much we have learned
concerning the spiritual and the meditative from China and
Japan. From an inevitable blending of East and West, an
important synthesis can result without the loss of identity.

In the future, there can only be an increased reliance of
foreign students on American schools with resulting interest
in exchange programs.

We are experiencing an increasingly beneficial influence of women in the fine arts. I reflect that all my own painting teachers were male and feel poorer for such a limitation.

The decades ahead will reveal hosts of changing student needs, the value of which must be weighed sagely by every faculty. As students lower themselves over building parapets to paint their designs, or attempt to distort architectural intentions by means of drapery, we must decide whether curriculums should change to reflect such interests and be able to distinguish between shallow vogue and the meatier stuff of "content."

To insure that the fine arts not be bypassed by educational change, art faculties should press increasingly to make art history and studio programs part of the university core curriculum.

A successful future for the arts demands a deep personal involvement on the part of those who teach, reflecting optimism and a joy in "doing." Any working program must display an honesty and a sense of excitement. There must be a clarity of purpose within the program and a strongly expressed philosophical viewpoint which can be easily understood by the student.

Certainly, in the future, there must be less institutional isolation. We can learn and gain strength from each other.

Rather than viewing the fine arts in American colleges and universities as at a watershed, it might be more correct to define the present situation as a cycle of change. Certainly, developments in the world outside the classroom are bound to be reflected within.

Recent economic cutbacks have severely affected both school enrollments and programs.

The commercial gallery situation has changed dramatically in this country since the lucrative years of the New York School. There has been a recent trend away from the exhibition of American painters. The current shows of the new European Expressionism are an example.

We have witnessed a shift of interest from the regionalism of the 1930s and 40s to the internationalism of the 1950s and beyond. Now there is a state of lull in the arts, a general sense of emptiness and lack of content. Many painters are returning to a more conservative, regionalistic attitude, thus completing the cycle.

A shift of emphasis has taken place from the public to the corporate buyer, now emerging as the new Medici.

Great leaps have been made in the field of art education since the first effort to establish an art school in Philadelphia in 1794. But, despite contemporary advances, much remains to be done. With full awareness of current difficulties, I can only exude optimism in considering the future of the fine arts in American schools.

Whatever develops in the arts, we as teachers and administrators must persist in spreading a simple truth: from Lascaux to the modern classroom, the fine arts are a challenging, inspiring, and noble profession.

Daniel Miller
The Pennsylvania Academy of
Fine Arts

ARCHITECTURE   In 1814, Thomas Jefferson proposed, for the first time in any country, that a professional curriculum in architecture be incorporated into a university program. This proposal was not developed in the University of Virginia, however, and only one course in the history and principles of classic architecture--which lasted only until the Civil War--materialized.

Essentially, before the Civil War, the few practitioners of architecture in the United States who had any professional training had gotten it in Europe; the only means of getting into practice in the United States was to apprentice in the office of one of the existing architects. During the first half of the nineteenth century, some of the technical problems relevant to the concerns of architecture were studied in isolated classes in such places as the Military Academy at West Point (1802); the University of Virginia, where civil engineering courses began in 1826; Harvard's Lawrence Scientific School (1847); Yale's School of Engineering; the University of Michigan (in the science curriculum); and Rensselaer Polytechnic Institute.

Architecture itself, however, was not established in American higher education until the Massachusetts Institute of Technology decided in 1865 to establish a professional course in the discipline and appointed William Robert Ware to plan and head this new curriculum (Weatherhead, 1941). Ware was a Boston architect who, after graduating from Harvard College, had studied in the New York atelier of Richard Morris Hunt, who had attended the Ecole des Beaux Arts in Paris and had enthusiastically brought back to the United States the principles and spirit of that institution. For two years after his appointment by MIT, Ware observed architectural training in London and Paris and made plans for the first American school. His courses opened in 1868 with four students. The program prospered and by 1875, there were 32 students.

The actual establishment of MIT (though the charter had been granted a few years earlier) was effected through the Morrill Land Grant Act of 1862. The next two architecture programs were also formed in land-grant universities. Cornell established a professional course of architectural study in 1871 as part of its College of Engineering, which was thereafter known as the College of Engineering and Architecture. The University of Illinois provided for a full professional course in 1867 and brought it to fruition in 1873. Then Syracuse installed architecture and painting as the two original departments in its College of Fine Arts, which was established in 1873. Five more schools followed before the end of the century:

- *Columbia University*
- *The University of Pennsylvania*
- *George Washington University (then called Columbian University)*
- *The Armour Institute of Technology (now Illinois Institute of Technology), in cooperation with the Art Institute of Chicago, which provided the drawing and design component*
- *Harvard University*

Of the architecture programs in these nine original schools, two were connected with fine arts divisions and seven were officially departments of engineering. The total enrollment in 1989 was 384 regular and 124 special students. By 1930, 53 schools, with a total enrollment of 4,575, were offering a full professional course in architecture.

The American Institute of Architects (AIA) was founded in 1857 to raise the standards of the profession. It immediately established a committee on education in which a great deal of discussion took place in the following years on curricula and policies. In 1912, through informal discussion at an AIA convention, the idea of an Association of Collegiate Schools of Architecture (ACSA) developed. That organization was founded in the same year to stimulate contacts between the schools and to establish informal educational standards through control of admission to its membership. In 1914, ACSA established "standard minima," but these were abandoned in 1932. In 1939, the National Architectural Accrediting Board (NAAB) was established to study programs at various institutions and to publish an annual list of approved schools. The board was specifically denied any power to standardize schools and was instructed to evaluate each program in its own terms.

It is not surprising that, when the impetus to establish professional architectural training in the United States developed, these programs were set up within universities, since it was the American tradition to center advanced training of almost any kind in these institutions. No doubt, these programs were usually assigned to engineering on the basis of a mutual interest in materials and building. Most architecture departments, however, found that being a subdivision of engineering was constrictive to the development of a well-balanced program in architecture and struggled to become independent units.

In the early years of the twentieth century, a compelling interest in design, often somewhat divorced from problems of construction and economics, developed in architecture on the campus. There was a burst of enthusiasm for the Ecole des Beaux Arts. American students went to Paris to study, and Frenchmen were imported to run the design programs in American universities. An American alumni society of Beaux Arts students was established which offered design competitions that became so popular that they practically dominated the methods and objectives of design teaching throughout the country.

From the very beginning, then, architecture in higher education was faced with the problem of integrating the various components of the discipline into a balanced and meaningful program of instruction and professional practice. It is by very nature a field that involves a wide spectrum of concerns and interests.

Architecture participated fully in the population expansion and growth in higher education during the twentieth century, experiencing the characteristic drop-off in growth and enrollment during the Depression. Today the ACSA, whose membership includes all degree programs in architecture, lists 87 full members in the United States. In their brochure, 1971/1972 Enrollments and Statistics, they report a total enrollment for 78 reporting schools (64 of which are accredited by NAAB) of 23,569 full-time students and 1,509 part-time students. The faculty for these schools is composed of 1,336 full-time and 1,033 part-time members, or a total full-time equivalent faculty of 1,687. During the past few years, approximately one new school has been added to the ACSA each year, and this growth rate is expected to continue. The U.S. Office of Education (1970) reports in Earned Degrees Conferred that in 1969-70 the following degrees were granted in architecture: 3,902 bachelor's degrees, 658 master's degrees, and 11 doctor's degrees. Not included in either of these sets of figures are the many courses taken by students not enrolled in a degree program.

Perhaps of all the arts in higher education today, architecture faces some of the most difficult problems. Integrating diverse components is an inherent problem for architecture, but the specialized concerns of the present are almost staggering in range and complexity: all aspects of planning; economics, especially banking; political science, not to mention politics; sociology; aesthetic and emotional needs; ecology; and, of course, engineering. The acuteness of the problems besetting our cities and the confusion engendered by rapid and often erratic changes make the architect's task even more perplexing.

Eero Saarinen expressed the idea that an architect always designs with the next larger context in mind, and some have extended this idea by saying that there are no architects today, only architect-planners. This direction of thinking, which relates a given structure to the nearest watershed as well as to the street it is on, brings the architectural problem to environmental design, a concept now guiding many schools. In any case, the social, economic, technical, and aesthetic aspects of architecture are currently subject to violent change, and both the complexity and the extreme flux in the field are frustrating to those who are seeking to manage its problems. (Consider, for example, the problems Saigon and its needs present today for the architect-planner). It is crucial, in such circumstances, that the aesthetic component of architecture be strengthened to contribute as vitally as possible to this effort. This is not a call for the architect to return to the era of the Parthenon or even of Sir Christopher Wren, but the conviction that, however the field develops, the aesthetic should be a strong component of the architectural-planning mix.

ARCHITECTURE
(Updated)

The act of inhabitation, though not celebrated in our time by its own Freud, must be one of the basic human acts, and making places comfortable for people to inhabit (visually, thermally, acoustically as well as spatially and conceptually), must be one of the basic human enterprises. Architects, since Imhotep at the very beginning of recorded history, have been in charge of making places, tombs (houses for the dead), temples (houses for the Gods), or even royal residences in which people's civic or imperial identification might be housed, and in the couple of centuries since the Enlightenment, and especially in our own time, it has become commonplace that the chief concern of architects is--or ought to be--providing spaces for people --not just kings--to live and work and play--to inhabit.

Unfortunately, we haven't quite learned how to do that, for all our rhetoric, and the questions of style, whether modern or post-modern, that seem to be central to most discussions of contemporary architecture don't even address our central dilemma, which is, I believe, that in the midst of our skilled composition of increasing numbers of architectural shapes, our cities grow increasingly hostile and unliveable.

What to do about it? What might the future of architecture hold? The choice, I think, is whether to follow the lead of the successful professions, like medicine and the law, to develop a body of "professional" information, increasingly inaccessible to the public, arcane, and expensive, or whether, more like the clergy, to loosen the profession, to open it to share with potential inhabitants the making of the physical environment, to try to tap the energies and images and memories of the people who will occupy buildings. That means that architects will have to learn to listen to people, and include them in the effort of making buildings and places, so that having helped make them, they can more easily find them habitable. That is the way I think we should go.

Charles W. Moore
Los Angeles

FINE ARTS CENTERS   Building complexes for the arts, usually called fine arts centers, have been growing in number since campus building programs burgeoned after World War II.   Two institutions in this study, Earlham College and Dartmouth College, are fine examples of schools which have arts centers that were designed and built to be an integral part of campus life.   John Sloan Dickey, former president of Dartmouth, was deeply involved in the development of Hopkins Center and was largely responsible for the placement of the campus post office and all student mailboxes in the middle of this fine arts complex.   This arrangement brings students, throughout their daily activites, within the physical environs in which artists are working, and in which galleries and concert halls are located (see note 10).   Runyan Center at Earlham is a combination student center and fine arts center.   A current problem in many schools, however, is the need to bring work done at the arts center into the curricular life of the university.   Also, just as scientists would not want their laboratories preempted by visiting colleagues, neither should artist-teachers have their own spaces turned over to visiting artists.

The idea of bringing the physical plant for the arts into the day-to-day life of the campus, often through combinations with other activities in readily accessible areas, is a sound one.   A special study of the nature and effectiveness of such physical centers for the arts is long overdue and would provide much useful knowledge for future planning.

Notes

10 The Henry Art Gallery at the University of Washington in Seattle was once on the edge of the campus and was usually one of the most deserted places there. When the campus building program established a new center of campus life in its proximity, the gallery began to teem with people.

FINE ARTS CENTERS
(Updated)

Building complexes for the arts, often called fine arts centers, continue to grow in number, as they have been since campus building programs burgeoned after World War II.

Two institutions in this study, Earlham College and Dartmouth College, are fine examples of schools which have arts centers designed and built as an integral part of campus life. John Sloan Dicky, a former president of Dartmouth, was deeply involved in the development of Hopkins Center and was largely responsible for placing the campus post office and all student mailboxes in the middle of the complex. This arrangement brings students, throughout their daily activities, within the physical environs in which artists are working, and in which galleries and concert halls are located. Runyan Center at Earlham is a combination student center and fine arts center, as is the complex at Washington University in St. Louis. Other recent examples of major arts facilities on campus include the Performing Arts Center at The University of Texas at Austin and The Krannert Center at the University of Illinois at Champaign-Urbana.

As colleges and universities have increasingly become centers of significance for American cultural life, the campus fine arts centers have faced specific and unique problems. First, the centers must be integrated into the curricular life of the university, a difficult task when faced with competing needs for limited resources. Second, the centers must find an appropriate balance between visiting artists or performing groups and the work of students and faculty in the arts. Third, the centers must discover--and at times actually create--their appropriate role in relation to other local community or professional arts organizations or facilities. Fourth, the centers must establish a sound fiscal policy, combining earned and unearned income with university allocated funds in order to provide effective financial management and control. Fifth, the centers must nurture volunteer organizations of both students and community persons. Finally, the centers face a myriad of other, perhaps lesser, problems, which range from public relations to development to ticket sales to facilities maintenance--in short, virtually all of the problems faced by any non-profit arts organization, made more difficult on campus because of academic responsibilites to curricular programs in the arts and to the institutions as a whole.

One thing is sure. Since World War II, fine arts centers have become a daily fact of life on many campuses, and the more elaborate ones rival the major cultural centers of the nation in size and scope. No special study concerning the nature and effectiveness of these centers has been conducted, though such a study could provide valuable information for future planning.

J. Robert Wills
Dean, College of Fine Arts
University of Texas, Austin

CULTURAL DIFFERENCES: AESTHETIC EXCHANGE IN ART EDUCATION

The practice of art education is intrinsically linked to culture, and hence to cultural differences. Culture informs both art production and reception. Western (print) art forms, for example, have dramatic and literary antecedents in the Artistotelian drama or in the post-Renaissance literary forms and differ in conception and execution from non-Western (oral) art forms that have folklore, legend and traditional spirituality as their antecedent. The print culture emphasizes individual originality, achievement and responsibility, while the folk tradition is governed by collective engagement and group competence. In the visual arts, we often see marked contrasts between private visual languages and a form of iconographic stylization expressive of the community's artistic norms. Thus, the immediate gratification phenomenon which is the end result of Western art is merely a stage within a folk tradition form in which the process of artistic elaboration is more important than the gratification offered by reception itself.

These approaches to cultural setting of art have deeper ideological implications which affect the teaching and appreciation of art. In terms of cinema specifically, films that hide the marks of production (those films characterized by technical brilliance and visual wizardry) are associated with the ideology of presenting "film (read 'art') as reality," i.e., art that announces its message as an "objective" reflection of the way things are. In such instances, spectator response is characterized by passive involvement, identification and acceptance. On the other hand, films that exhibit the marks of production (roughness of style, slow pacing and repetition of images) are associated with the ideology of presenting "art as message," i.e., film that announces itself as a polemic comment on the way things are and not their "natural" reflection. Spectator response in this case is characterized by active involvement, "distanciation" and interrogation of the filmic message. These conventions of conception and presentation can be reversed in the structure of a specific art form, the variation in style being only meaningful in the context of use. Because non-Western art advances a specific cultural and/or historical message, it is structured to invoke an ideological point of view which recognizes art as a cultural message.

The resistance to each other of the two differing modes

of artistic discourse is a natural outgrowth of the unequal exchange which has historically been tilted in favor of the West--the West as the privileged observer and communicator and the non-Western as the observed and the receptor. Now that the West is in the position where it has lost the privilege of being the decoder of messages, it has to reexamine the role of art in a given society. The shift in the make-up of Western thought born out of the desire to overcome a cultural fixation with itself has created the need for a self review, not only of its own conventions but also of how it regards "art" from other cultures. Coupled with this is the non-Western's desire, particularly those of the Third World's, for self-reliance in the cultural domain and a reexamination of its art on its own terms. The fusion of these two factors has brought into sharp focus the necessity for a meaningful dialogue and the need for a cross-fertilization of ideas. The perennial problem of cross-cultural communication must not any longer be relegated to a peripheral academic interest. The awareness of viewing art forms as noteworthy and meritorius, despite cultural and/or geographical distance, is deserving of greater attention and occupies the center of a genuinely rounded art education precisely because we cannot afford to dissipate a store of knowledge which is the key for a peaceful cultural coexistence.

The domestication process of incorporating art forms from other cultures shorn of their signficance, that has characterized Western education, must finally, therefore, give way to a new start and a fresh perspective. The future maturation of a synthesis between the two modes of artistic expression should lead us toward a dynamic aesthetic confluence of a more meaningful cross-cultural/ideological exchange. This trend, which is coming into its own in most disciplines in the Liberal and Fine Arts, under the rubric of a semiotic inquiry into the meaning of art, is a most deserving scholarly pursuit and will be a healthy augury of what the future holds.

Dr. Teshome H. Gabriel
Department of Theater Arts and
Assistant Director, African
Studies Center
UCLA

DISCUSSION

Students

In the 1973 edition of my report to the Carnegie Commission of Higher Education (see note 11), I offered an ad hoc classification in five parts of undergraduate majors in the arts:

1. Students of strong commitment
2. Students who are honestly "shopping"
3. Students who want a general education with an arts major
4. Students who "minor" in the arts
5. Students who are "showboats"

Although the percentage of those entering higher education as freshmen whose "probable field of study" (see note 12) is 4% (about half the number entering the arts twelve or so years ago), it is still a healthy figure compared to english (.9%) and history (.5%) but down from "business administration" (general) at 7%. The characteristics of these students, I am told, generally follow my five-fold ad hoc classification of 1973. The difference between 1973 and 1983 students may be suggested by an often repeated statement, "They (the students) are serious, hardworking and practical (lots of "commercial art"), but they should be more daring."

Some students design a life-style for themselves which will support them with "food, shelter and clothing" and time for their work in their chosen arts. One young man is a carpenter three weeks a month and a sculptor the fourth week. Some join or create their own gypsy companies.

It is clear that even during a recession with a severe "economic crunch," the number of young people interested in pursuing the arts is substantial.

Resistance to and Support of the Arts

According to reports and my questionnaire to the sixteen selected institutions (see Appendix F), resistance to the arts in academe has reduced and support has grown. The scattergram of Appendix C, however, indicates that the arts must extend their relationship systematically to include campus-wide contacts as well as the community at large.

Rate of Change in the Rise of the Arts

It's plain that the "rise" is leveling off. Since the arts
are still relatively new to academe, there may still be a
slight rise or perhaps a broadening of arts penetration of the
campus.   But it is strongly suggested by the data on the
questionnaire that a leveling is occurring. This is due to
some major institution setting quotas to control admissions.
The "numbers game" has been won. Quality is now the major
challenge.

Notes

11 Morrison (1973)

12 The American Freshman National Norms for Fall 1983 by
Alexander Asten published by ACE and UCLA. (Four percent is
the sum of "Art, Fine and Applied,: Music, Theater, Drama" and
half of "Arts and Humanities").

3
Seminar Results

On October 2-4, 1983, UCLA served as host to a national seminar to discuss the topic: ARE THE ARTS ON CAMPUS AT A WATER-SHED? Following, is a summary of the roundtable sessions including questions and responses by seminarians and audience participants. The chapter closes with a review and interpretation by the author. We plunge into the myriad points and observations from the seminar.

Traditionally, the arts were understood to be a trade or craft and their teaching was delegated to an academy, a conservatory, or an institute, while the university dealt mostly with conceptual knowledge and the advancement of <u>ideas</u> in learning.

In 1957, Sputnik was launched and the United States went into competition with Russia on all fronts. Suddenly, our universities were charged with advancing science and technology to an almost unreasonable degree. At approximately that same period, the NEA was established and we began building cultural centers and, after years of appeal, brought these centers into the universities. It was, in a way, demonstrating that we, too, have a culture, while we were demonstrating our concern with high technology.

Since 1957, what has happened on all fronts is phenomenal. When one considers the attendance at all art events in the U.S., including museum visits, live performances, etc., there is a greater yearly population than at all athletic events combined.

71

DISCUSSION OF SEMINARIAN'S REPORTS

Once, the arts represented very rich alternatives in our society. In our own country, they symbolized a spirit of creativity, and, if you went to art school in Indiana or Louisiana, or New York or on the West Coast, you felt a sense of place--a commitment to regionalism. That commitment to regionalism brought to the main centers in the U.S. new alternatives, so that when a dancer like Ray Bolger would bring his country way of dancing to Broadway, he introduced something new. Now, instead of regionalism, we have a kind of off-off-off-off Broadway, so that one of the problems in the state of the professional arts is that there is nothing new being brought into them. What is difficult and troubling today is that our arts programs in universities are mirroring the professional world, and in effect, we are training people in planned obsolescence.

One seminarian asked, "Where is the evolution occurring or going to occur when theater is looking to the university for professionalism and the university is looking to theater to model professionalism as evidence of why the arts belong in a university." Where, she asks, is research going to occur and new theater evolve?

One respondent sees the Yale Drama School as modified by Bob Brustein in the 60s as the new model for professional theater on campus. Research, she feels, will be basically connected to the present, with the key researcher being the literary manager. This key person will research new plays, new trends, and in addition, will provide the director, the artist, and the designers with basic information for them to look to the present. In other words, the intent of present theater is not to replicate how one used a cane on stage in 1660, or how to use a cane per se. They will provide that information, but more important is making old works appear unfamiliar and strange. Only a brilliant director can perceive modernistic trends in very old works and make them visual and oral for the contemporary audience, she added.

Still, there are those who do not believe the university can accommodate both professional theater and conservatory training programs. Others see the university as a very important umbrella, and liken it to a museum or a library and not a commercial entity. To those, it is a facility that combines professional theater with conservatory training.

All seminarians agreed that it is better to have a separate College of Fine Arts than to be a division of the College of Arts and Sciences. Feeling persists that a dean with too many disciplines would not consistently argue in favor of the arts. Whatever the format, all see a need for spatial proximity and formal interchange of ideas.

On the subject of professionalism, there was unanimous support for heightened student commitment and competency. Several speakers favored a move to deny degrees to students who did not reach prescribed competency at the graduate level. It was shared that in the MFA program at one school, there were several stages of mid-year evaluation, and then, promotion was by yearly invitation only. There were reminders that the university supported three levels of training, each with its own goals and restraints. The undergraduate level is a tempered one that simply defines the major; then, there are breadth requirements. Before one is accepted to graduate programs, there should be audition and recruitment of such high quality that attrition could be avoided. Seminarians did agree that the Ph.D. degree program was being eliminated in some schools in favor of strengthening the MFA degree. Common feeling is that universities cannot successfully offer a BFA and a MFA in theater without the MFA being of lesser quality. In summary, all discussants applaud the broad-based liberal arts degree with 10 or 12 classes in the arts. Once students are weeded out for a graduate program, naturally, the concerns are different.

Dance people showed great concern about choreographic content in general, lack of choreographers, and lack of teachers of choreography. Even in professional dance companies, choreography is considered to be thin. It was agreed that at the university level, the dance department should have a company on campus, but not one that is allowed to grow so large that it becomes almost unrelated to the department's original intent. (Companies begin with limited week-end performances but invitations grow; teachers must find substitutes to replace them in class; jealousies and other problems occur.)

An obvious question was raised: If a person wants to dance, why doesn't he or she join a dance company? Why does one need a college degree? How does one equate school and dance? Do you say, "Please come to college and build your mind as your body is beginning to decline"? The university feels a definite responsibility for the post-dancer. But more important, there is agreement that the gifted, but very young dancer would not have the intellectual capacity to build a foundation for that gift--and that very quickly that dancer might exhaust the fascination she or he holds without the intellectual foundation to build on. In particular, the university is seeking the dancer with a "discordant personality"--that rare combination of talent and intellectual curiosity. The university is right only for those who seek intellectual development; The conservatory is better suited for those who want just to dance, or sing, or act.

Voice development has as much to do with physical maturity as with intellectual maturity. One respondent, in particular, felt that not every college or university should have a voice program, but that a university that wishes to take that lead should excel, the way Juilliard excels, and be a balance between conservatory and university training. One of the disappointments this speaker found with today's universities is that they are too performance oriented. Speakers from several other disciplines agreed, calling this "getting there before you get there." Instead, some feel, the university should be teaching performance assimiliation, language training, coaching, and even contract negotiation. Moreover, it was said, a singer must have a broad-based liberal arts education and must be aware of the interrelation of the arts. (One cannot be an introverted singer and be successful.) In some professions, there is a qualifying examining board--not so in the arts. For this reason, there was strong feeling that teachers never let a student misconceive that he is good.

In total, the mission of the university is to train and refine and prepare. The university that wants a successful voice department must take that extra step toward building a reputation. For example, for those would-be professionals who are out in the world and are as yet unsuccessful, bring them back into the academic fold at the graduate level. Reinforce their abilities in language, dance, acting, auditioning and negotiating skills. Make the university a career builder so that the successful graduate and professional can applaud his or her university and, at the same time, attract dedicated and talented undergraduates to a winning university with a proven record.

When contemplating study in any of the arts, one always wonders where to begin--how to handle the past. In painting, as in other disciplines, it is necessary to begin at the beginning. It is important to avoid that feeling of casting the past aside. Even the abstract or non-realist artist must

be skilled in the basics. Increasingly, exhibitions are calling for and including drawings for the paintings for display
along with the end result.

Too often, students are tempted to emulate a style that's
currently popular. The tendency, however, is to do this
repeatedly, when there is no personal foundation to build on.

For those who teach painting and other visual arts, there
demands an extra degree of personal involvement--a constant
reinforcing of excitement, mood, and optimism, and a continual
struggle between fad and content.

Seminarians agreed that the 80s will foster a spiritual
sharing with Eastern cultures and the arts will blend into
"one world."

Extraordinary possibilities exist today to create images
that only a few years ago would have been unthinkable or
prohibitively expensive to process. But these advances have
raised pedagogical questions for teachers in the Motion
Picture/Television area. Where does student training start
today? To what extent can one "play" with the medium rather
than go through the rigorous training into these new areas of
expression? There is an obvious concern with the degree of
prior knowledge needed to assure one's growth potential.

With so much concern for technology, one seminarian was
tempted to ask, "What about the human connection?" MP/TV has
two areas of concern: production and criticism. Their needs
are both individual and overlapping, but there is definite
interaction. Whatever the technology, unless one is dialoging
with a certain tradition...filling possibilities of that
tradition or moving beyond it--and it must include some awareness of the historical, the critical, and the theoretical
dimension of the media within which you are working--that
technology is an intense dialogue between the creative people
on the one hand, and the people concerned with history,
theory, and criticism on the other. They should not and
cannot exist in total isolation from one another. This, one
expert said, is where the research excitement is today. The
world of film criticism has rediscovered history with a
capital H.

At least one seminarian felt that purely academic recognition of creative writing reached its peak a decade ago. Today, the usefulness of an MFA or a Ph.D. in that field has
lessened because it ceases to be marketable. On the other

hand, it is believed that all major universities and most 4-year colleges <u>are</u> offering adequate and well-attended courses in creative writing.

For the hopeful writer, where should the university's role end? Perhaps the most important aspect for the young writer is the ability to meet and speak directly with a published or publishing writer who is willing to take time to review and frankly discuss a student's work. One new kind of involvement that is supported by various colleges and universities are writer's conferences. These seminars are held weekly or monthly to discuss marketability, agents, publishers, and audience. Some university conferences feature writers-at-large, who are available to students for criticism and advice on their work.

Poetry, collections of short stories, and first novels are the least publishable works even in good financial times. Where does the role of the university end? Unfortunately, little change is envisioned into the 1980s and 90s unless the university further recognizes and ultimately publishes its own student and faculty works. If the university is ready to fill the gap opened by the decline of commercial publishing, the government will often provide start-up money toward that end--but certainly they will not remain yearly patrons. It's hard to be a writer--you don't get much help.

Roughly, there are 200,000 students majoring in the arts at universities at any given moment--that is, 200,000 of our 11,000,000 students (see note 13). Dare we insulate and isolate these 200,000 instead of allowing them to present themselves to their contemporaries as dancers, actors, writers and artists? If so, 10,800,000 may still graduate from a university in American without exploring and without discerning the beautiful from the ugly.

It isn't the responsibility of the university to engage in local politics. But when visiting universities in Gainesville, Georgia, or New Mexico, for example, and one is surrounded by pollution and visual slums, it becomes at least arguable that these enclaves surrounded by squalor suggest that the university is not playing its full role in preparing the majority for citizenship in that country in which the environment is playing such an important factor.

Organizations like the J. Paul Getty Trust are pioneering and have successfully brought the arts into our primary and secondary schools. Presumably, that will encourage genera-

tions of students with an aesthetic awareness into our universities.

We have concentrated upon the role of the university in
training professionals. We agree that two generations of
growth and expansion have been accomplished. Professional
opera companies have grown from 27 to 68; theater companies
from 12 to 66; symphony orchestras from 58 to 120; professional dance companies from 10 to 134. It is obvious that the era
was part of a worldwide movement. Similar growth was shared
by England, Australia, Canada, France, and many other free
countries. We can distinguish five elements in this expansionist era:

1. Sympathetic technology in electronics broke down
barriers and made the arts accessible.
2. Increased appetite for the arts in a substantial
segment of citizenry.
3. Increased ambition among artists. This is in direct
contrast to attitudes of artists of the 40s and 50s who
communicated only to a narrow circle. In the 1980s,
there have been measurable attempts to reach a wider
audience, provide greater services, and play a larger
role in society.
4. We had an expansionist view of government. (It was
not only held by populist leaders such as Lyndon Johnson,
but by conservatives such as Richard Nixon as well).
5. An expanding economy sanctioned this expansionist
view of government. The surplus in the national gross
product enabled government to carve out new functions
such as support for the arts and for education.

The result was a substantial increase in the numbers of
citizens who identified themselves as artists. (Information
gathering is unsystematic and statistics are likely to be
faulty.) Roughly, in 1975, 823,000 Americans identified
themselves as artists. In 1982, that number had risen to
1,129,000; actors increased from 20,000 to 37,000 in that
period; authors from 47,000 to 71,000; dancers from 8,000 to
18,000; designers from 135,000 to 233,000; musicians from
151,000 to 160,000; artists and sculptors from 155,000 to
219,000 (see note 14). (By no means can it be assumed that
all people are earning a living in the profession with which
they have identified themselves.)

If the figures are significant, and even moderately
reliable we are adding to this large body of Americans who
call themselves artists, another 60-70,000 per year.

If the universities feel responsible for their graduates, how are they obligated in maintaining a balance between ambition and opportunity, between supply and demand? The Arts Endowment moved backwards into this realm. Without any reflection or preparation or any precedent, it established a series of programs that worked well during that period, and in effect, provided the working capital for expansion without interference or censorship. The role of the government during this period was creative and limited. It was also without foresight and was marred by internal contradictions.

The contradictions between programs supported by federal government were obvious. Under pressure, our government subsidized the end product in the arts, and ignored the education arena, which was clearly the key to creating a favorable climate in the future. It set out to replace instead of reinforcing the existing arbiters of taste and talent. Only lip service was given to the principle of decentralization, but in all critical questions or aesthetic judgments, the power was in Washington.

In this new time that we are in, it is necessary to return to the five elements which fostered earlier expansion and to review them. The sympathetic technology remains. The appetite for the arts remains, and with it remains the desire of artists to draw an audience. Government is doing what it can to make the economy dynamic again, and Americans would applaud a disposable surplus. In the meanwhile, what exists is disillusionment, along with a pledge from both parties that they will begin to limit the role of government.

Those who sponsored creation of the Endowments are gone from government: Hubert Humphrey, Jacob Javits, Clayton Pell, Frank Thompson, John Brademas, and Sidney Yates, who is near retirement. Employment is down, opportunities are down, and performing arts is the hardest hit. Dance is suffering from the demise of the touring program. (Travel costs make touring expenses prohibitive and many smaller companies are approaching bankruptcy.) In spite of the need there is still no national policy. Instead, the NEA goes on, year after year, endorsing the arts in ways that the government sees appropriate. Neither innovation for the arts nor wisdom in funding is built into that structure. At best, NEA support is a means of buying time.

In general, a considerable degree of artistic vitality is showing signs of erosion due to economic and institutional pressures. Commercial theater has become a victim of sharply

rising costs.   On Broadway, both production and weekly
operating expenses more than doubled between 1975 and 1981--a
rate of increase half-again higher than inflation in general.
Higher costs lead to inflated prices and inevitably, there has
been a steady retreat from artistic risk-taking and increasing
stress on sure "hits" from audience and producers alike.

The nonprofit resident theater movement is scarcely more
than twenty years old.   It was begun in a state of high
idealism by talented artists who wanted to work with a continuity and seriousness of purpose not possible in commercial
theater.   Sadly, practical details of day-to-day management
increasingly have created a gap between these ideals and their
achievement.   In addition, major sources of support such as
the Ford Foundation, the Rockefeller Foundation, and the Arts
Endowment have limited their support.   One final realization
is that under the goals and guidelines of nonprofit theater, a
dignified future is problematic.   Here again, few would disa-
gree that the university should be the pivotal agency.

The mission for the 80s and beyond is clear.   The arts
must be placed in the context of dialogue with broader areas
of knowledge, for example, linguistic analysis as it applies
to film text, or business management in relation to art
patronage.   This is an important function that distinguishes
the university from other training agencies.   The University
must expand and clarify its roles as a patron of the arts, as
a trainer, and as a producer.

Seminarians, and others, continue to applaud the basic
American approach to education--that every kid should have the
chance to try to be what he/she wants to be.   How many hope-
fuls actually enter medical school, or receive veterinary
training?   Early identification is fine, but no one should be
denied the opportunity to try.

In sum, the goals of a university are education, research, advancement of knowledge, and service to the public.
In addition, the university continues to be a balance between
ambition and opportunity, and supply and demand.   Continually,
these centers of learning have taken on new involvements
concerning audience development and marketing the arts.   Both
these interests are part of an interrelated pattern that
fosters and reinforces research.

One speaker referred to the university as an "inner-
space," a hub in a flow of communication, where a multitude
of fields intermingle and a dialogue is carried out between

the arts and sciences that intersects with the public. Certainly, any formula that joins university and audience in partnership will lessen anxiety and promote positive hopes for the arts, students, professionals, and amateurs, alike.

Notes

13   Approximate numbers were supplied by a seminarian and past Deputy Chairman of the NEA.

14   See Footnote 13 above.

FINDINGS

Ideas, observations and individual experiences produced many
lines of discussion, but on reviewing them, a pattern appeared
with ten segments. They are offered here with the observations that could be subsumed under each segment of the
seminar:

Administration

Under this rubric, a number of thoughts, questions and
agreements occurred:

    a. It was agreed that the arts in higher education had
had become, for the most part, an integral part of the
academic scene and were in a maturing process which put
their future in the hands of the arts leaderships on
campus.
    b. Who is (or should be) the educational and artistic
leader in the departments of the arts in higher education?
    c. The astute and aggressive use of academic diplomacy
is vital to the maturity of the arts on campus.
    d. A number of knotty problems remain such as the bi-
furcation of a department into the academic treatment of
an art and the practical treatment of making art. The
academic side is a horizontal, collegial operation and
the producing side is vertical and hierarchical. (One
possible way this problem is being met is by designing a
department with those two operations working side by
side.)
    e. The understanding and commitment of the faculty to
the department's "mission statement" is seldom found in
arts departments. Further, it is important their mission
statement be understood and accepted by the community on
and off campus.
    f. Scale and the mission of the individual institution
often dictate policy as an extra-curricular, co-curricular (see note 15) or curricular approach to administra-
ting the arts on a 2-year community college campus, a
4-year liberal arts college, a comprehensive university
(to the masters level) or the major research university
with doctoral programs, post-docs, and research institu-
tutes.
    g. A dynamic concept and program to contribute to

general liberal arts on campus is vital. As one of the major ways to teach the symbols of culture, the arts have a great responsibility.

h. The institution could become a major broker for the arts in the community by administering government funds, putting artists in the fields where commerce has failed (chamber music groups, gypsy dance and theater companies, for example) and contributing to the development of local, state and federal policy for the arts. The campus could serve as an "umbrella" for the arts.

i. The institution could clarify the concern over using the arts as a learning tool in education, instrumentally, rather than an art in its own right. It could do this by creating a "School for Public Aesthetics" or "School of Artistic Health" which would use artistic processes (drawing, improvising drama, dance and music, for example) by teaching their processes in learning our symbolic culture.

j. The arts on campus have a responsibility to monitor "the individual vs. the establishment problem," seeking a balance that will serve both effectively.

k. Higher education must continue to define and clarify its role in the arts. For example, its work as patron, producer, teacher, researcher, policy-maker etc. needs constant attention.

l. The endemic question of quality vs. the "numbers games" needs constant surveillance and useful answers.

m. As an interface with all disciplines, the arts have a special responsibility to society for making knowledge useful.

n. The "College of Fine Arts" is proving to be an effective administrative unit for the arts on campus. A dean of such a college has only the arts to serve rather than myriad departments of the sciences, social sciences and the humanities.

o. Many of the major research universities have served the arts very well but the special role and responsibility of the major research university has not been addressed.

p. The future of the arts in higher education lies in the hands of its educational and artistic leaders on campus today along with those professionals in the arts who will find common cause with those on campus.

Educational   Philosophy   (more   thoughts,   questions   and agreements)

a. The university is for talented students who also have an intellectual curiosity--a so-called "discordant personality." The conservatory is for those who only want the arts.
b. The university is a patron of the arts.
c. The university goal is to turn out artists.
d. The university carries out its traditional service to the arts with teaching, research and public service.
e. The university must define its role in the arts.
f. There is not a major discontinuity between the arts and technology.
g. There is a need to define what modernism and post-modernism may mean for teaching the arts in higher education.
h. The artist has always dealt with new technology.
i. The new technologies have never hit the arts with such an impact as they have today. The moving image (motion picture/television) is particularly hard hit with state-of-the-art equipment hard (expensive) to come by.
j. The university is not interested in commercial arts but in the "advance guard."
k. MP/TV faces the terra incognita of technology and attempts to humanize it.
l. Totally independent (one person) creativity is not possible in MP/TV--and theater, dance?
m. Is there synthetic art with collective creativity?
n. The arts are in the service of the community. They have a social responsibility as taught in the university e.g., national policy.
o. Technology and the poet is an endemic condition.
p. The post-doc level of development is critical.
q. The "skilled amateur" may be the key future "product" of the arts in higher education.
r. Contemporary humanizing of the culture is primary (access: is it elitist or egalitarian?).
s. Small press organizations are a sine qua non for the development of writers.
t. What is the proper balance between professional demands and individual student development?
u. What is the appropriate time for student artists to undertake public appearance?

Research

a. Conventional 19th century Ph.D. research in the arts
is dead.
b. Performance theory, anthropological oriented research
is alive. (Observe the "literary manager" in theater.)
c. Research in the arts must be re-defined--whither
research?
d. What is the proper balance between serving the
student and serving the field?
e. Is "story telling" still the core of the artistic
statement?
f. The ecology of the artist is still to be dealt with.

Pedagogy (mostly questions)

a. How does one teach the route towards development of
the coupling of maximum freedom with maximum discipline?
b. How does one teach "feeling" and "experience"? (Are
there some lessons that can only be self-taught? A
teacher may set up situations in which the student may
make or develop his own discoveries.)
c. How does one learn to retain "the resonance of human
experience"?
d. How does one learn the relation of process to end-
product?
e. Craft without feeling is "the empty technique."
f. Understanding what one is doing precludes "the empty
technique" and focuses on the audience.
g. Avoid boredom.
h. Humanizing the arts is the work of the artist.
i. Working with professionals at a professional level is
a must for world-class artists.
j. If gut teaching isn't possible, gut learning must
develop somehow. Working with "feeling" or developing
"the gift" is still obscure--but present.
k. Individual differences must be recognized and dealt
with--as with "natural talent."
l. Access to the profession is a constant shifting
problem to be faced. "Post-docs" are needed in this
limbo of career entry.

Marketing

    a. "Getting a job" is a collateral but important aspect in the education of an artist. His eyes must be opened to the condition of "the market" for young people in the arts. How is the young artist supported?

    b. "Career entry" for the young artist is a growing concern and the responsibility of education and of society at large.

    c. The effect of "the marketplace" on academic matters is a fact which cannot be shrugged off. The relationship of the artist with his audience (however defined) is a vital one for the artist and our society today. The worst of commercial conditions for marketing the arts exists across the country. The young artist spends an inordinate amount of time breaking into and dealing with the marketplace even after a successful "career entry." One observer has said along with others that "it will take the university to blow this ⌈marketplace problem⌉ open."

    d. One reasonably effective way for young artists to meet the problems of career entry and the marketplace is the "Gypsy Company" for dance, theater and music. The "Small Press" is an analogous operation for the writer as is the intimate gallery for the visual arts. Colleges and universities could go far in supporting this concept.

    e. Building bridges, developing avenues to a re-defined marketplace should be a prime target for arts management.

    f. Learning the ways of "the profession" and how to meet them must be on the young artist's agenda.

Funds and Fund-raising

    a. In light of "the economic crunch," fund-raising and reallocation of funds is a major problem to be met.

    b. A question of far-reaching implications is "what is cost-effective in the arts?" The industrial model won't do.

    c. By taking small wages, performers support the arts.

Curriculum

> a. Audio-visual literacy is a requirement in today's world.
> b. Overlaps, one department with another, needs special attention--not to make clean breaks but foster effective relationships.

Recruitment

Recruitment, whether of faculty or students, must seek out "the discordant personality," that is, a personality that is talented and motivated to seek out both the artistic and intellectual life on campus.

The Chair

The chair of an arts department has dual responsibilities: educational and artistic leadership. Can such a person exist?

Innovations

An "Institute of Advanced Study in the Arts" is a must for major research universities to provide extra-departmental growth, a place where inter-arts efforts, experiments and studies of all kinds can develop in an arts environment where power is vertical and hierarchical.

Notes

15 Between the extra-curricular program in the arts on the American campus and the conventional university department, there is an emerging administrative entity which may be called "co-curricular." This emerging entity takes various forms. For example, the small (1,000 students) four-year liberal arts college usually has a faculty "adviser" for each of the arts from the faculty of each arts departments. The University Dramatic Society (UDS), a student enterprise at Oxford and Cambridge in England, is "amateur," but, in the theater, professionals like Peter Brook, Jonathan Miller and Peter Hall have emerged from UDS. It gives one pause to think!

SEMINAR PERSONNEL

MILLY BARRANGER - Theater; University of North Carolina,
  Chapel Hill

JOHN ESPEY - Poet; Topanga Canyon, California

DOROTHY MADDEN - Dance; Paris, France; London, England;
  Martha's Vineyard, Massachusetts

DANIEL MILLER - Painter; Pennsylvania

BOB ROSEN - Film Archivist; Los Angeles, California

MICHAEL STRAIGHT; Bethesda, Maryland

WILLIAM WALKER - Baritone; Fort Worth, Texas

ROBERT H. GRAY, Host - UCLA College of Fine Arts, Dean

MOLLY MAGUIRE, Recorder - UCLA College of Fine Arts

JACK MORRISON, Chair - UCLA College of Fine Arts

4

Observations and Recommendations

NO MAN WHO COMES TO KNOWLEDGE THROUGH ART LEAVES THE
FEEL OF WHAT HE KNOWS BEHIND, FOR THE KNOWLEDGE HE
COMES TO, IS THE KNOWLEDGE OF THAT FEELING--"LIFE OF
THE MIND" WHICH COMPREHENDS BY PUTTING ITSELF IN THE
PLACE WHERE ITS THOUGHT GOES--BY REALIZING ITS
THOUGHT IN THAT ONLY HUMAN REALIZER--THE
IMAGINATION.

IT IS FOR THIS REASON THAT THE TEACHING OF
POETRY--OF POETRY ITSELF--IS SO IMPORTANT TO THE
UNIVERSITY IN CRISIS, AS IMPORTANT AS THE TEACHING
OF SCIENCE AND, PERHAPS, WHEN THE WHOLE COLUMN CAN
BE ADDED UP--MORE IMPORTANT. FOR ONLY WHEN POETRY
ITSELF, WHICH MEANS ALL THE POWERS OF ALL THE ARTS,
REGAINS ITS PLACE IN THE CONSCIOUSNESS OF MANKIND
WILL THE TRIUMPHANT CIVILIZATION WHICH SCIENCE HAS
PREPARED FOR US BECOME A CIVILIZATION IN WHICH MEN
CAN LIVE, ALIVE.

Archibald MacLeish
1961

THE AUTHOR"S CONVICTION . . . IS THAT MUSIC BEGINS
TO ATROPHY WHEN IT DEPARTS TOO FAR FROM THE DANCE;
THAT POETRY BEGINS TO ATROPHY WHEN IT GOES TOO FAR
FROM MUSIC . . . .

Ezra Pound
1934

OBSERVATIONS

In the interest of making more informed, if not wiser, decisions about the arts maturing in academe and their effectiveness and in the interests of society, students, faculty and the arts themselves, I am offering some observations and recommendations for what they may be worth.

Like medicine, science, business administration and social sciences, the arts had to fight their way onto the American campus. Hardly impetuous, the academic establishment was slow and deliberate in accepting the arts on their own terms over the last 200 years or so.

Now, however, favorable popular opinion prevails and the arts are generally accepted by many administrators in academe and by informed laymen. This block of opinion maintains that the arts are no longer outside looking in but are an integral part of the academic scene. (See Appendix A for a listing of those interviewed.)

Faculty and administrators in the arts on campus can no longer afford the comfort of a paranoidal view that they are still in a persona non grata status in academe. Quite the contrary--the others on campus expect those in the arts to stand up to the academic condition as a full-fledged member of the establishment. The arts are, at last, mature members of the academic family and are expected to behave that way.

This point-of-view, a fresh one, leads to fresh developments for the arts which must be considered.

First an axiom: Strategy for the arts (or any academic discipline) can be discussed from a national position but tactics (curriculum, courses of study, recruiting special personnel, budgeting in specific terms, for example) are only possible institution by institution and, therefore, will not be discussed. After a mission statement is made, strategic decisions, naturally, will affect the decision about tactics mightily. Now about the strategies.

Salient Strategies

The first strategy is not a new one--but one that is even more powerful than generally thought. It's the venerable power of recruitment, both faculty and student. The clearest, most forceful "mission statement" might as well be written on water if the faculty and students are not already consciously or unconsciously committed to the direction that statement puts forth. Someone who has been committed exclusively to the classics is quite likely to continue that way. He is not likely, at least in the near future, to commit himself to the production of new and original plays, for example. And students who do not already have a well-developed intellectual curiosity are not likely to commit themselves to the intellectual side of the curriculum in a way that's productive to him/her or the work at hand.

It seems to me that the instructor is the curriculum. If he/she doesn't embolden the teaching, no manner of course description, syllabi or discriminating reading lists will help the student achieve mastery and creative control of the course material. One can speculate why this is so, but a fundamental point is that an artist's work springs from his holistic, authentic self.

Recruiting in the arts is not served well by paper. From this point-of-view, the best recruiting can be done by going to centers where prospective artist-teachers are likely to be found and by getting into the professional and social mix of the young, talented pool of people in a given art. Then one can see them at their work and evaluate the personal and professional make-up of the likely ones who would be interested in the academic, artistic life. In cities like New York, Los Angeles, San Francisco and Chicago, there are sub-cultures of young artists, some of whom are ready for the academic life having proven themselves professionally. Moreover, many of them not only have baccalaureate degrees, but masters and doctors as well.

A student's academic record is pretty standardized and hardly studded with information about his/her promise of talent in a given art. But leading schools in the arts all demand (in addition to grades, SAT scores etc.) interviews, auditions and/or portfolios. Such a procedure not only helps screen a student but indicates what kind of a lash-up he is getting into. The arts are what artists do. From discussions with students, it's certainly clear that the well-motivated, spirited and talented student seeks out those institutions who do offer interviews and auditions around the country every year. And they seem to know very well who went where the year before--and for what reasons.

The emphasis falls on recruitment because it's the creative individual--in a creative environment--who makes art.

The arts on campus will only go as far as the individual creative teacher and student will take them. Books are important generally and particularly for the arts. But an artist cannot leave his "formula" in a book for others to follow. He can impart the spirit of that "formula" or, more likely, share a stimulus which will help others develop their own "formulae." Therefore, recruitment becomes a vital force in developing faculty and students for a virile, vital and productive department of the arts.

Excellence - (what else?)

The second, but equally valuable, key force in the arts is quality (excellence). Perhaps one should say the pursuit of excellence and quality. Who isn't for quality and excellence? It's the excitement of the pursuit of these two values that can permeate a department and stoke engines of creativity. That pursuit, with attention to quality, can lead to excellence. People who say that everything they do is "excellent" can't be very discriminating. Even among people like Picasso and Shakespeare, there have been "pot boilers." Some of their works are better than others. But pursuit of top performance as an artist is constant.

Mutual Respect

The third force--and probably the most chimeric of the three--is collegiality--true, professional collegiality. Assembling a faculty and student body that "gets along" professionally is more productive. Backbiting, subversive criticism in the hall, rather than forthright but supportive eye-to-eye criticism which creates a supportive demand for excellent work, is enervating. The myth that the most creative are the most horrid must go. It helps continue a vicious, destructive "publicity gag" that's gone too far. This doesn't mean that conflicts are out or that heated differences must disappear. It does mean that combining collegiality with good recruitment and high quality work equals more effective, creative work and more effective teaching.

The collegiality I'm talking about is the kind of collegiality Lipshitz wrote about which he, Picasso, Braque and a few others shared in Paris during their youth. At Sunday breakfasts, they held what could be called a roving seminar when they talked about the poetry reading of the night before--or a ballet or symphony. The ensuing dialogue generated ideas of great fecundity. The opportunity for such

collegiality in the arts on campus has never achieved the
level it could achieve (see note 16).

Currently, I detect an amorphous feeling that "we should
be more interested in each other and each other's work." This
amorphous feeling, interestingly enough, includes more than
colleagues in the same department, it includes the other arts
and the rest of the university as well. If this "amorphous
feeling" grows to become strong enough, the artist-teacher-
colleague will make time for it. He'll never find time for
it. And it will pay off to the artist-teacher and avoid the
worst excesses of parochialism. The stimulation of colleagues
throughout society and the world is great for the working
artist.

This sense of becoming more engaged with one's
environment--artistic, social, economic and political--tracks
along with an emerging view that "art for art's sake" is dead.
Art for the community's sake is coming alive--not in the old
sense of "social realism" as Stalin and Hitler had it. But in
the sense of an artist responding to society in his own
idiosyncratic way (see note 17). This doesn't mean the next
great epic poem challenging Childe Harold is likely to be "Ode
to the Exquisite Washington Budget Delay." It does mean that
the artist who speaks to his community will be the one who not
only survives but is likely to grow in artistic stature, like
Sophocles, for a neat example. It may be instructive to
recall that Lorca was accepted as a "great Spanish poet" not
only because he wrote poetry for the "little magazines" but
composed ballads that were never written down but "picked up"
by the peasantry who just liked them as good songs to sing.
Suppose the members of the audience were considered to be
colleagues?

An Instructive Analog for the Arts: The Teaching Hospital

An idea floated out by Eric Larrabee some years ago likened
the operation of the arts in the university to that of the
teaching hospital. The analog isn't perfect, but it is
instructive. Look at the forces at work.

The medical staff practices as well as preaches (teaches)
medicine. The professional practitioner is the key to the
system. He/she has a double task. The teacher (often called
a "clinical professor") is as much concerned about the
library, the research, and the admissions program as he is
about caring for a patient's health. His commitment is to
all. He has to involve himself in university affairs (tenure,

promotion, administration) as a member of the faculty. The student is involved with classes, research, and student life as much as he/she is concerned with becoming a medical doctor.

This approach gives the lie to the hoary aphorism, "He who can, does; he who can't teaches; and he who can't teach, teaches preachers." The teaching hospital, at various levels of success, does not consider the faculty member a split personality. Rather, he is an integrated personality with a unified pattern. The pattern suits individual differences by means of various balances of practice, teaching, research and service to the campus and to the local, national and international community. It's not for everyone.

Though working imperfectly, the lesson to be learned from this analog is to take on the problem of finding and/or developing such personalities rather than setting up a series of false "either/or's" (doctor or teacher, artist or teacher). Even though some faculty members will emphasize research more, let us say, rather than practicing, teaching or community service, he will understand and respect the need for a balance of responsibilities in a teaching hospital.

It appears to me--at least in major arts programs in major research universities--that such a model would be extremely useful in developing and maintaining an effective arts faculty and a student body of university stature. Some artists do enjoy teaching and "practicing." Those who don't need not apply. There is genuine excitement for those who combine practice, research, teaching and community service. It's a full-time job if ever there was one.

The "New" Department

After spending over a half-century becoming academically decent by imitating other academic departments such as english, history, zoology or philosophy, a department in any of the arts now faces the task of becoming a department of the arts on its own terms. A music or theater department, for example, must become a place where student and faculty artists may thrive, a place where the ambiance, in addition to spaces, equipment and financial support, carries a spirit that stimulates and encourages the "creative leap." There is an air, an aura, among people who are working artists that is catching. Developing into a true arts department may well be the most significant challenge to the arts in academe today.

These three points--recruitment, quality and collegiality

--can be considered major variables in the operation of departments of the arts on campus. If those three forces are driving well, the department should be superior. But there are some "minor" variables, critically important in their own right but not quite as powerful as the three major forces. Here they are (in no particular order):

Promotion and Tenure

Promotion and tenure continue to be a nagging problem for the arts, probably more than other departments in a college or university. It is of particular concern as this is written, because in some departments fresh personnel are locked out for the next twenty years. What does one do about the promising, young and talented artist or scientist who goes stale after ten or twenty years? One useful method for departments who already have the tenure system is offered in Appendix E. Another tenure plan is a modified contract system. A new member, for example, is hired on a five-year contract renewable in the third year. This gives reasonable security to the faculty member and two years to adjust, if his contract is not renewed for another five years. In any case, a department that does not face the problem of tenure and promotion directly is likely to stagnate, a condition as dangerous to faculty as it is to the students they work with. The one-year contract and lecturer status are other means of dealing with the tenure problem. Although this is a way of gaining time for decision-making and is working in some places, it is probably "stalling" and creates a condition that is enervating and destructive to bold, spontaneous, creative work. Professional sports (baseball, football and basketball) have developed systems that reward young talent, and players are not thrown on the "dump heap" when they no longer deliver top performance. True, they have more money to work with, but something may be learned from them. How do you retire "over-the-hill" talent with respect and financial support? This puzzle has no easy solutions but ignoring it will not make it go away. Unanswered, it may mean slow death for some departments. Locked-in faculty positions are the most serious threat to quality because it cuts off fresh blood for the department.

Stick with the Pros

Dance (modern) on the campus probably has the best relationship to the professional world among the arts because modern dance as art was introduced at the University of Wisconsin, Madison in the 20s by Margaret D'Houbler, who studied with the pros in New York. Martha Hill brought a similar relationship to Bennington about that same time. Some observers think that the future of dance in the university will be determined by the force with which the campus stays in touch with the professionals. Certainly the same story, told in different ways, is heard among all the arts. "We have to stay closer (or get closer) to the professional world of our art." How to do it is the trick. After a number of failures (measured by the contribution of the campuses to the students), theater departments now have resident professional companies on about a dozen campuses. Witness University of North Carolina at Chapel Hill and University of Montana at Missoula. In any case, a "leading" department must be judged from a "World Class," professional point-of-view.

Correlative to this problem of how to relate effectively and positively to the professional world in each art is the sub-problem of how faculty members may practice their art among peers of "World Class" (see note 18). (It's interesting and provocative that Nobel Laureates in the sciences characteristically have Ph.D.'s in their fields. But to date, a Ph.D. in literature has not received a Nobel prize in literature, according to reports.) Some campuses located in or near big metropolitan centers encourage their faculty to work professionally even while they are in residence.

And it works the other way as well. One world class scenic designer could not make a living if he did not have an appointment on the faculty at Yale. Many faculty members have felt a kind of sibling rivalry with their peers in the professional world, but this seems to be diminishing. Certainly parocialism must go. (One university theater scholar got promotion and publication for a quarter of a century writing on the "hate Broadway" theme.) Many reason that the "uppity" stance by academe is on its way out.

Institutionalizing

Or how to bureaucratize without being bureaucratic. This is one of the current major topics for the Graduate School of Business at Harvard University. To keep an operation going--a dance department, a gallery program, or an oil company--you make it into an "institution." But how do you do it without strangling it with orderly procedures on the one hand or chaos on the other? At one point, the Comedie Francaise, institutionalized to preserve the genius of Moliere, was strangling him to death. If you wanted to see something funny and telling, you didn't go to the Comedie Francaise! How do you keep the Guthrie Theater in Minneapolis solvent or the Museum of Modern Art without a Guthrie or without a vibrant artistic director? There is no handy manual to guide you through this problem. It's under study, but it is unlikely that a useful formula will ever be available. The trick is to find a balance in a given, special, artistic venture, which weighs orderliness and accountability with artistic freedom and daring. Institutionalizing--or the opportunity to achieve it--depends largely on a community of thought (whether on the campus or the wider community--local, state, federal, international) where the "institution" will live. That, in turn, means the arts need statesmen who will provide a small "p" political platform for the arts. Statesmen like Beverly Sills, Michael Straight and Franklin Murphy.

Anthropological Approach

Performance theory couched in anthropological terms is gaining increasing interest not only among anthropologists, but artists. (The Wenner-Gren Foundation is funding such research.) And it may be out of such studies of the ritualistic use of the arts which may show the way the arts as arts serve the community rather than exist for the old-fashioned notion of "art for art's sake." The shaman, for example, is a prize subject in this field. His/her performance may be "pure dance" or ritual in service to the tribal chief--or luck in war or in love. Ignoring performance theory may be injurious to the artist's health.

Disciplinary Splits

Musicologist-composer, art-historian-painter, theater critic-playwright, scholar-artist--what a bloody scene! But it's a scene whose unity, coherence and structure is marred by composers and musicologists who do work together without anger; painters who take art historians to lunch and directors whose best friends are critics. What to do? Currently, one campus has seen the art historians break away from the art department to be on their own. Maybe this is the best way to go--in some local situations, it's the only way to go. If there are but two basic functions in the field of the arts, they are (a) making art and (b) encountering art. Logic would seem to relate these two functions to each other. The differences are personality differences rather than incompatible, fundamental differences of function or method. A reasonable response to the problem is to say, "stay tuned!" Bennington is committed to the compatibility of artist and scholar. Maybe size and specialization account for that.

Scale

Scale may be a critical factor in the way the arts may or may
not work on the campus. One student at Earlham (student body
of 900) was a triple major: theater, psychology and German.
What chance would there be for a triple major of any kind at
any major research university? There is no "right" or "wrong"
here. It does mean that scale (size of student body, classes,
studio work, production and performance) is critically important. If a music department, for example, is going to have
performance groups, an optimum size of student body or faculty
must be determined. This is a critical point in determining a
mission statement for the music department. Space, naturally,
is linked to faculty and student body size. How big is big
and how small is small must be defined for each department and
for the function of the institution as a whole. (Whose eyes
are bigger than whose stomach)?

The Technology Flap

Most, if not all, responses to the question, "How is the impact of current developments in technology affecting the arts
and the teaching of the arts?" were along the line of "what
else is new?" The point being that the arts have always faced
new developments in technology. Whether it's with pigments
alone or printing of all kinds, or the moving image on film
and/or tape, dealing with new technologies has characterized
the artist's existence down through the centuries. And the
current impact is, in concept, no different today. True, the
current impact is undoubtedly deeper and wider than ever
before, but a poem is still a poem no matter how expressed.
Somebody has to be a poet before his/her poem appears in line
and color, texture and sound, moving choreographed bodies,
film, or on tape. It is here that the university arts program
is most practical because it may be more aware that the ideas
(concept, drive, or need for expression) come first whatever
the technological challenges are. This can best be construed
as making a case to ignore the new technologies and their
impact. Quite the opposite. A big danger now, because of the
economic crunch, is that the equipment and materials of the
new technologies may not be available for student and faculty
to exercise in his pursuit of expressing his artistic idea.
Just as physicists need increasingly sophisticated equipment
to pursue new knowledge, so does the artist need state-of-
the-art equipment and materials to pursue a fresh expression
or a new mode. The damage of the economic crunch is vicious
in a subtle sort of way in these instances because a depart-

ment may have a fine faculty, reasonably good pay, good space and an alert student body. But if state-of-the-art equipment, materials and supplies aren't available, the development of contemporary technologies just isn't possible.

Economic Hazards

The hazards of the economic crunch tend to be hidden rather than obvious. And the hazards are likely to reach their peak in '85-'86. All university departments are hurt by the lack of fresh, young, vital talent. The arts are probably more vulnerable than other disciplines since fresh, new work depends almost solely on the artist. As mentioned elsewhere, state-of-the-art equipment, supplies and materials seriously limit the opportunity to master the new technology.

An economy of scarcity almost always brings out the worst in mankind (some "primitive" tribes excepted), and a good deal of energy goes into puerile sibling rivalry instead of the work at hand. The counseling of students in times of duress points them toward "something you can make a living at." This isn't bad advice for some students and faculty members, but, if the USA is going to continue to be the "land of unbounded opportunity" for our young people, the opportunity to try any career (pre-med, pre-law, math, or professional athletics, as well as the arts) must remain in force and receive full funding.

Marketing the Talent

It's curious that parents, the establishment, friends and other well-wishers counsel students away from the arts, though the opportunities in them may exist at better odds than in pre-med or professional athletics. Even the military academies do not graduate 100% of the freshman class in four years. Attrition has its effect across the board. The odds of "making it" in the arts are not good. But the youth in our society who are talented and motivated should, with full knowledge of the odds, be able to give it a shot. An under-graduate major in the arts is provided a good general educa-tion and, after a student gives his first career choice his best shot, he can use his education in varying ways in related or unrelated careers. Somehow, the general public must be educated to this point-of-view in fairness to themselves and to their young. Many parents under 35 years old are beginning to have the view that young people in our society should have the opportunity to pursue the first of their hearts' desire.

In sum, artists do not develop the same way accountants or carpenters or merchants do. They have to find their own idiosyncratic way (with patient, helpful guidance) in their development and in marketing themselves.

Outside Funding

Outside funding (that is, money from sources other than the regular institutional budgeting process) usually comes from six sources--individuals, corporations, foundations and federal, state and local agencies. Individuals, regularly, account for the largest grants. But any effective program providing funding will take on all six routes. Government agencies will likely eschew "high risk" projects. Federal funds generally go for "Research & Innovation"; state funds for institutional support and capital improvements; local support for community projects; and individuals, corporations and foundations for what appears to be in their personal interests (or guidelines developed by a Board of Directors or managers).

At minimum, the systematic pursuit of outside funding is at least a full-time job for one person. The minimum unit of time in building a program is three years and efforts should include face-to-face visits. Funding sources need to know who is being funded, as well as what and how. It is sound practice to use institutional money for operations and outside funds for projects. Beware of "soft money." There are, of course, many variables affecting a fund-raising program. Raising money for a major research university is one thing. Raising it for a public two-year college or a private, old-line, 4-year college is another. In any case, any innovative and/or research efforts are likely to depend on outside funding in the near and far future. The arts unit on any campus should not be without a "Friends of the Arts" and an appropriate fund-raising program.

Methods of Teaching

With all the current talk of "the new technology" and innovative teaching, there doesn't seem to be any radical change from the current approach of many good institutions at present. That approach may be described by three points: (a) providing and orchestrating the seminal uses of the past, (b) providing a sound base in the craft of the art, and (c) providing an environment in which each student is helped to find his/her way of working. (No gurus)! Each must learn how to plumb his/her source of originality. Whatever the "Zeitgeist" or technological impact may be, at anytime, putting the individual student in an environment wherein he may thrive is the function that remains constant (but not stale!).

Arts Events from Off-Campus

Often, if not always, the campus is the cultural center for the community for off-campus arts events as well as those developed on campus. Galleries, concert halls and theaters for exhibits, concerts and shows are often the only exhibit and performing spaces available. In fact, some campuses such as University of Illinois-Urbana, University of Texas-Austin, Dartmouth and Autonomous University of Mexico, have arts centers which challenge New York's Lincoln Center. They are, however, a mixed blessing. Who gets first-call on the facilities? Who gets what billing and money? How can the programs from off-campus and on-campus supplement and complement each other? And how can the administrators of both avoid empire-building and adult/sibling rivalry?

In large operations on big campuses where both have their own space rather than mutually-used space, the best plan seems to be to let them go their own ways. But in an institution of higher education, such a laissez-faire point-of-view may be entirely out-of-sync with the on-campus views of the arts. But, then, the campus entrepreneur points out that his/her presentations are for the community and are not extensions of the classroom. Devices for meeting this problem vary from campus to campus, but the basic principle for cooperation is a vehicle in which both (or all) parties are represented by people of good will (there are some!). One practical problem is that most on-campus events are planned with 12-15 months lead-time and off-campus bookings are liable to be 18-30 months lead-time. But these are matters which must be dealt with specifically, institution by institution. (Perhaps the greatest danger is to have someone handling the off-campus events who is out to emulate the late great entrepreneur of the peforming arts, Sol Hurok--on university money). One fundamental postulate which applies is that the academic demands of faculty and students come first in awarding time and space. Quality is the next big question, but persons of good will who know their business can develop a cooperative, mutually serviceable program. A secretariat to accomplish this coordination is indispensible.

The Steady State

In our world today, much has been said in many quarters about the loss of American vitality because a "no-growth" view is accepted after the loss of our "frontier." The result, some people believe, is stagnation, death. It seems to me that the "steady-state" is the practical answer because a steady-state depends on dynamic balance in an inner and outer world today. A "normal" temperature of 98.6°, in a human being, for example, is the result of a very dynamic process as anyone who has hit a temperature of 94° or 104° will tell you. Maintaining that "steady-state" of 98.6° is anything but stagnation. The arts on the campus can deliver this point to society. And, certainly, if we look at work in the arts, the work of the artist is constantly of a dynamic nature whether the "frontier" has vanished or not. The artist hasn't a boundary and is in the position of being "lost" completely if he doesn't find his way on the edge of his own, exclusive untrammeled "frontier." Furthermore, this leads to a final speculation.

The Century of the Skilled Amateur

The only frontiers left to American society for the 21st Century are those frontiers each individual chooses for himself. And a challenge available to all is to choose one of the arts and pursue it as an amateur. This could destroy the nation entirely. The loathing of the amateur by the professional is rampant and often well-deserved. "Amateurish" is a derogatory term of great distinction.

But this well-deserved ephithet does not apply to the skilled amateur. The highly regarded, greatly revered American composer, Charles Ives, lived and died an amateur leaving an American heritage in music that is priceless--and gaining in stature. Adolf Appia, "the father of modern scenography" changed scene design for good, yet he is reported to have designed only six productions in his professional life, four of them in living rooms. Nathaniel Hawthorne was a rank amateur when he wrote The Scarlet Letter. Sophocles was a statesman and a general, not a professional writer, nor was he a member of the Dramatists Guild. Being "professional" does not automatically assure distinguished work, or any work at all.

The arts in higher education have the great opportunity to contribute to the national talent pool of skilled amateurs. Community theaters, orchestras, dance groups, filmmakers, arts

centers, schools and galleries all stand to be bolstered by
the skilled, talented and motivated amateur. To achieve such
a development, faculties will have to give up their put-down
of the amateur and distinguish between "amateurism" and the
endeavor of the skilled amateur. There are many men and women
in the work force who would be thrilled to pursue the art of
their concern if they could work with other skilled amateurs
rather than the terrible tyros who have given the genuine
amateur a bad name. (Such a point-of-view also helps
ameliorate the "marketing" problem. Those artists who don't
"make it" in the "real world" would have a respectable place
to work.) Be that as it may, there are portents and signs for
society and individuals which indicate a future for the
skilled and talented amateur.

Correlative to the above is the question of arts in
education (sometimes called aesthetic education) in our
schools. There has been much palaver about this matter and
lots of smoke blotting out any substantial fire. "Purists"
say this is watering down the arts, vulgarizing the arts.
Well--if such vulgarization is similar to what Luther did when
he "vulgarized the Bible" so as to make it plain to the
people--as in the marvelous King James English version--then I
am for "vulgarizing the arts!" But this would not be at the
cost of neglecting the artist and distinguished work at a high
level of excellence. Perhaps "arts in education" should have
the same relationship to the artist as a school of public
health does to the exquisite art of the neurosurgeon in a
school of medicine. Both the elite of medical practitioners
and the workers in public health have the same general goal
--preserving life and contributing to the health of the
community. But they take different routes with different
responsibilities to accomplish the common goal. They do, in
fact, complement and supplement each other. The relationship
is cooperative rather than adversary. As someone has said,
great artists need great audiences and great audiences need
great artists. But, more than that--each individual in our
society must have the opportunity for relationships. They are
vital to effective education in the arts on campus.

Additional Observations

Where the arts on campus are found to be thriving, they are
more likely to be in an administrative unit such as a college.
Fifty years ago, it may have been necessary to ride on
someone's coattails. In fact, being a separate department
reporting to an established academic dean, vice-president of
academic affairs or the president himself, was often more

supportive and flexible than being lumped in with the other arts at the time. But that condition seems to be over. Scrambling to survive or just to stay even with the game of financial and administrative support on a department basis is no longer effective. Moreover, such isolated departments in the arts are beginning to seek out each other--to cooperate or compete for space, funds and promotion. Departments already together in an administrative unit appear to be more successful, sailing under their own colors and setting their own artistic standards on artistic principles.

Is There a "Growing Edge" or a "Cutting Edge" in the Arts?

Great stock is taken in the academic world to the term, "growing edge" of knowledge or the "cutting edge" in the realm of advancing knowledge and discovery. They are respected for good reasons. Advances in knowledge, and in civilization, have come for those who dare work on the growing edge of knowledge or the cutting edge of a discipline. Such terms are highly respected in the sciences, the social sciences, the humanities and the professions--but! Are they appropriate for the arts?

The arts are different. While an artist in any field does use previous knowledge and techniques, particularly in learning his craft, does the mature artist stand on the "growing edge" of his art? Does he have to find his way to the "cutting edge" of his art? If so, where is it? Is it necessary to map out the terra incognita before "doing," making a "new work?" Is a painter forbidden not to do another Madonna and Child because someone has already opened and closed the field of Madonna and Child the way Helmholtz did optics in his day?

The analog to growing edge and cutting edge for the arts may be a "fresh" rather than simply a "new" work. New developments seem to explode rather than "grow." The artist explodes in some kind of holistic fashion. There were no lines around the terra incognita behind which "Da-Da," for example, lurked. Painters exploded with the idea in action. Picasso, Braque and the others picked it up and the Armory Show of 1913 proved every critic "wrong." The artists were "right." The critics were busy writing about "schools" and trends and who was "hot," but the painters were painting.

This view need not be labored. It's only worth our attention in academe because the work for the artist cannot be understood on terms other than his own. There is a need for an understandable analog to the work of scholars and scientists if the artist is going to be an integral part of the academic scene. There still prevails a notion on the part of many scholars that the artists are "Mickey Mice," who merely play at fun and games. And, if the discursive symbols of the scholars--words and numbers--are the sole measure of the artist's work, they do come off as Micky Mice. But if non-discursive symbols (see note 19)--color, line, sound, beat, moving bodies and moving images--are used as additional ways of knowing, the artists' work comes off as very serious, as "import" laden with values on its own "scholarly" terms.

How can judgments, then, be made? By the time-honored academic way: peer judgments.

What still has to be clarified, carefully explained, and established is that of an "artistic method," the analog of the highly respected "scientific method."

Notes

16 (Well hardly ever! There have been reports of effective collegiality from the early days of Black Mountain and Bennington. Undoubtedly, at some other places like Earlham College. But the great opportunity for collegiality is too often missed.)

17 It's almost too pat but Picasso's Guernica and Anouilh's version of Antigone produced in Paris during the German occupation are obvious examples.

18 CILECT (The Centre International de Liaison des Ecoles de Cinema et Television [International Center for Cinema and Television Schools])

19 The terms discursive, non-discursive symbols are those of Suzanne Langer.

RECOMMENDATIONS

1. Now that the arts are a recognized unit within academe, it is imperative that their administrative structure in departments be built to arts needs rather than parrot what is perceived as an "academic department."

2. Each department in the arts must have an educational and artistic leader who provides an understanding and responsibility to both the degree-granting function of the department and the production side of the department in an effective manner.

3. The arts should see to it that they become an independent administrative unit of top management or administration within an arts college or division (depending on the local administrative structure).

4. The arts should take on their position as an "inter-face" with other disciplines.

5. The campus should be a major broker in community arts affairs.

6. The university should face the problem raised by the arts being utilized as a learning tool and symbol-making force in society. Perhaps a "school for public aesthetics" could take on this challenging task.

7. Technology and the poet (particularly in Film/TV) pose an endemic challenge. Currently the challenge is great and the ability of the poet to master technology is being tested.

8. The arts should champion inter-disciplinary research to describe and de-mystify the ecology of the artist.

9. Each department must avoid the danger of "The Empty Technique"--Teaching sterile craft without any passion.

10. Recruitment of professional "discordant personalities," intellectual and talented in the arts, which fit the opportunities in the arts in academe, must become a conscious, deliberate administrative tool for selecting both faculty and students.

11. The arts should teach how to employ maximum freedom together with maximum discipline.

12. The arts must open new avenues to a re-defined marketplace which will serve to provide the artist with sensitive
feedback on his own terms as well as provide a commercial
market for dollars. The industrial, commercial model does not
fit the artistic needs of artist and audience. Presently
neither the mature artist nor the student deep in the state of
career-entry are well-served.

13. A useful and potentially effective administrative device
of great extra-departmental power is an institute for advance
study in the arts, or, as noted previously, a kind of "R & D
Center" for the arts. Whether this develops as a professional
theater company in the theater department, a professional
chamber music group for music, a wild-cat gallery for visual
arts or "gypsy company" for dance or something else doesn't
matter. What does matter is a high-level working relationship
with professionals.

14. Departments must increase the traffic, by whatever
effective measures, with the professional world of the arts.
Vacuums in the arts are non-productive. "Masters" in each are
vital to developing student standards.

15. The 21st Century will be the century of the skilled
amateur -- skilled amateur, not the tyro. Our society, as has
been wisely noted, will have more and more product coming from
less and less employment. More members of our society than
ever will need something to do to make life worth living.
Higher education in the arts can help provide meaningful
activity for our people by educating and training skilled
amateurs. These amateurs would be of the stature and pro-
ductivity of Ives in music and Appia in theater.

16. As noted in # 6, there is a problem of bifurcation in
utilizing the arts as teaching tools: although both schools of
medicine and schools of public health are concerned with the
health of human beings, their work is quite different. Although epidemiology and garbage disposal, for example, need
not be the direct professional concern of the skillful neurosurgeon, garbage disposal is a deep and serious concern in
schools of public health. It's simply a matter of division of
labor. More people will have good health if both do their
jobs well--and respect each other's worth.

A similar situation may exist in the arts. The exquisite
artist (Beethoven, Shakespeare, Picasso) need not drop his/her
work to teach fourth grade solfege or to manage the next fund-
raising drive for the city arts council. The sculptor should

not drop his hammer and chisel to pour the concrete for the new sidewalk even if more people use sidewalks than use neurosurgery.

What is useful here is a new thought, a thought which will bifurcate the arts along functional lines similar to the differences between the surgeon and the fieldworker in public health. Both are necessary and useful.

The differences may be seen in the protest by some artists or some critics of the arts: the protest is against using the arts instrumentally in teaching, using the arts as a teaching tool. This, they say, is watering down the arts, or, even worse, destroying them. My suggestion is that we should not confuse the instrumental use of the arts with the intrinsic value of the arts, by making and encountering the arts as phenomena in their own rights. Perceiving the inner and outer world through the senses is fundamentally the same process for artists and all the rest of us (see note 20). It has probably been good pedagogy during the life of man to use the arts instrumentally in teaching and religion. There should be another name for learning by using the arts as symbols, of ways of getting to the child with non-discursive symbols, in sound, dramatic play, color, line and moving bodies, perceived in various frames of mind. The word "non-discursive-symbols" carries the message. (But it has too many syllables. It needs a good, old-fashioned anglo-saxon word. Vibes!)

Whatever that word turns out to be, the current need is to recognize and respect the basic similarity and the basic difference between the discursive (words and numbers) and the non-discursive. Both are needed and one should not threaten the other. Man, the symbol-making animal, needs to use them all to provide the kind of understanding which will serve school, society and the world effectively.

To build such an institution in which the word "arts" would not be used but would feature sensual function of the human body to teach the symbols of our society with all the senses operating, there should be created a "School of Public Aesthetics." (A working title.) Learning by perception through all the senses can foster this use of what we call the arts as an instrument of learning.

No doubt there will be "gray areas"--thank goodness!

17.   The arts establishment in higher education should

undertake a careful study of itself. "Growing like Topsy" is often the most effective growth. (Topsy was an interesting and attractive little girl who was pretty sure of herself). But growth has introduced a clear perception that the arts are not a monolith of goals and objectives. The arts programs, for example, in a small liberal arts campus and the programs in a major research university may both be excellent but quite different. Future research in the field must be fractionated but not become reductionist. For comparative purposes, there are at least four classes of institutions: 2-year college, 4-year liberal arts college, comprehensive university and major research university.

The Council of International Fine Arts Deans has taken a step in this direction with their support of the HEADS project. It's a critical and well-planned first-step to provide base-line data. But what can develop without waiting for HEADS to develop a respectable base is to introduce case studies of comparable campuses. The condition of each category of the five institutions are complex and diverse enough to deserve special treatment. With the growth in size and internal conditions, the budgets of the arts in higher education are understandably larger and administrators deserve good data of a quantitive and qualitative nature. Offices of internal institutional support must take on the arts as part of their charge. Those in the arts must give such offices the nature of data in the arts and insist on a mutual development of what will be accepted as good data.

18. The overall administrative structure for the arts unit on campus should be "The College of the Arts" with "Schools" for each of the arts rather than departments. The "Schools" would have "Directors" rather than chairs as educational and artistic leaders:

What's in a name?

The recommendation above is not a cosmetic one. It meets the previously unmet dichotomous demands of the collegial, horizontal structure of the departments in Letters and Science on the one hand and the hierarchical, vertical, professional demands of production and studio work on the other. This sort of structure makes it possible to set up an operation which recognizes the idiosyncratic function of the arts and artists and relates them to the academic function on their own terms. Currently, on most campuses, the chair of a department may or may not be an educational and artistic leader. Ad hoc oligarchies and despots spring up without direction or accounta-

bility clarified and with the spoils of confusion and squab-
bles locked in.   This kind of structure, a college with
schools, identifies and clarifies responsible educational and
artistic leadership.   (Who wants to fly in an airplane piloted
by a committee?)

Notes

20   See Rockefeller Jr., D. (1977).   Coming to Our Senses

Selected References

Ackerman, J.S. (1973). "The arts in higher education." In C. Kaysen (Ed.), Contents & context: Essays on college education, New York: McGraw Hill.

Anderson, J. (1972). Untitled notes, Athens: Ohio University.

Barron, F. (1972). Artists in the making. New York: Seminar Press

Boas, F. S. (1914). University drama in the tudor age. Oxford: Oxford University Press.

Council on Higher Education in the American Republics. (1964). The arts and the university. New York: The Institute of International Education.

Dennis, L. E., & Jacob, R. M. (Eds.). (1968). The arts in higher education, San Francisco: Josey-Bass.

Fowler, C. (Ed.). (1980). An arts in education source book. New York: The J.D. Rockefeller 3rd Fund.

Gardner, H. (1983). Frames of mind, New York: Basic Books.

Graham, K. L. (Ed.). (1966 November). "The relationship between educational theatre and professional theatre: Actor training in the U.S." Educational Theater Journal.

Harvard University Report of the Committee on the Visual Arts. (1956). Cambridge, MA: Harvard University.

Hausman, J. J. (Ed.). (1980). Arts in the schools, Chapter One with John Goodlad and Jack Morrison, New York: McGraw-Hill.

Langer, S.K. (1953). Feeling & form, New York: Charles Scribner.

Langer, S. K. (1958). The cultural importance of the arts. Lecture delivered at Syracuse University, reprinted in Philosophical sketches, Mentor Books, New American Library, Inc., 1964. (Originally published in M.F. Andrews (Ed.), Aesthetic form and education, Syracuse, NY: Syracuse University Press.

Lewis, A. (1972, February 5) "To grow and to die": III, New York Times, op-ed page.

Lowry, W. M. (1962, May) "The university of the creative arts." Educational Theatre Journal, 14, 99-112.

Lowry, W. M. (1978). The performing arts and American society, Englewood Cliffs, NJ: Prentice Hall.

MacLeish, A. (1961). Personal communication. (Original source unknown).

Madden, D. (1972). Untitled manuscript, University of Maryland, College Park.

Madeja, S. S. (Ed.). (1978). The arts, cognition and basic skills, St. Louis, MO: CEMREL, Inc.

Marks, J. E., III. (1957). America learns to dance, New York: Exposition Press.

Matthews, A. (1914, March 19). "Early plays at Harvard." Nation, vol. 98.

Mahoney, M. (Ed.). (1970). The arts on campus: The necessity for change, Greenwich, CT: New York Graphic Society.

Meltz, N. M. (1971a, July). Patterns of university graduations by field of study in Ontario, Canada and the United States, 1950-51 to 1968-69. Institute for Policy Analysis, Toronto: University of Toronto.

Meltz, N. M. (1971b, August). Projections of university graduations by field of study in Ontario, Canada and the United States, 1969-70 to 1980-81. Institute for Policy Analysis, Toronto: University of Toronto.

Morrison, J. (1973). The rise of the arts on the American campus, New York: McGraw-Hill Book Company.

National Association of State Universities & Land-Grant Colleges. (1979). The state of the arts at state universities & land-grant colleges. (NASULC), Washington, D.C.

National Research Center for the Arts. (1975). America and the arts: A survey of public opinion, Associated Councils of the Arts, New York.

Novotny, J. A. (1981). Role conflict and accord: The artist and the humanist in the university, Center for the Study of Higher Education, The Pennsylvania State University, University Park.

Perkins, J. A. (1965, July 17). "Should the artist come to the campus?" Saturday Review, pp. 54-56, 70-71.

Pound, E. (1934). ABC of reading, New Haven: Yale University Press.

Presidential Task Force on the Arts & Humanities. (1981). Report to the President, The Superintendent of Documents, U.S. Government Printing Office, Washington, D.C.

Quincy, J. (1860). History of Harvard University, Boston, vol. 1: (Publisher name not available).

Rice, N. L. (1972). Untitled manuscript, Carnegie-Mellon University, Pittsburgh.

Report of the Commission on the Humanities. (1980). The humanities in American life, Berkeley/Los Angeles: University of California Press.

Rockefeller, D. Jr. (1977). Coming to our senses. A report by the arts education and Americans panel, New York: McGraw-Hill

Stake, R. (Ed.). (1975). Evaluating the arts in education. Columbus, OH: Charles E. Merrill

Stillings, F. S. (1972). Untitled manuscript, Central Michigan University, Mount Pleasant.

Supper, A. A. (1979). A climate of creativity: The founding and development of a school of the arts, The Golda Meir Library, University of Wisconsin, Milwaukee.

Wallace, K. R. (Ed.). (1954). A history of speech education in America: Background studies. New York: Appleton-Century-Crofts.

Weatherhead, A. C. (1941). The history of collegiate education in architecture in the United States. A Columbia University doctoral dissertation, published by the author, Los Angeles.

Wing, C. W., Jr., & Wallach, M. A. (1971). College admissions and the psychology of talent, New York: Holt, Rinhart and Winston.

Wright, C. D. (1967). "A Survey of the creative writings and writer-in-residence programs." Proceedings of the Sixth National Conference on the Arts in Education. National Council of the Arts in Education, Pennsylvania State University, University Park.

Appendices

APPENDIX A

LIST OF INTERVIEWEES AND SEMINAR PERSONNEL

The list of people interviewed for this report spoke fully and freely. They were candid. And while they influenced my thinking deeply, they are not in any way responsible for the positions I've taken in this book.

JAMES ACKERMAN - Harvard University; Cambridge, Massachusetts

JAMES APPLEWHITE - Duke University; Durham, North Carolina

WILL BARNET - New York

MILLY BARRANGER - University of North Carolina, Chapel Hill

FRANK BARRON - University of California, Santa Cruz

BERNARD BECKERMAN - Columbia University; New York

GRANT BEGLARIAN - National Foundation for the Advancement of the Arts; Florida

STEPHEN BENEDICT - Columbia University; New York

GARRETT BOONE - Earlham College; Richmond, Indiana

JOHN BRADEMAS - New York University; New York

ANDREW BROEKEMA - Ohio State University; Columbus, Ohio

RAYMOND BROWN - University of California, Los Angeles

SUSAN BURCAW - University of California, Santa Cruz

ARLENE CLIFT - Fisk University; Nashville, Tennessee

MARTHA COIGNEY - International Theater Institute; New York

DOUGLAS COOK - Pennsylvania State; University Park, Pennsylvania

DONALD CRABS - University of California, Los Angeles

TAYLOR CULBERT - The Ohio University; Athens, Ohio

ALFRED DE LIAGRE, JR. - American National Theater Academy; New York

LANNI DUKE - J.P. Getty Foundation; Los Angeles, California

SEARS ELDREDGE - Earlham College; Richmond, Indiana

PAULA FAULKNER - University of California, Los Angeles

WINONA FLETCHER - Indiana University, Bloomington, Indiana

GLADYS FORD - Fisk University; Nashville, Tennessee

HENRY GOODMAN - University of California, Los Angeles

HANNA GRAY - University of Chicago; Chicago, Illinois

ROBERT H. GRAY - University of California, Los Angeles

BRIAN HANSEN - University of New Mexico; Albuquerque, New
  Mexico

ADRIAN HARRIS - University of California, Los Angeles

MELVYN HELSTIEN - University of California, Los Angeles

ROBERT HOLMES - Pennsylvania State University; University
  Park, Pennsylvania

LEONARD HOLVIK - Earlham College; Richmond, Indiana

MICHAEL HOOKER - Bennington College; Bennington, Vermont

SAMUEL HOPE - National Association for Schools of Music;
  Reston, Virginia

LONNA B. JONES - The Rockefeller Brothers' Fund; New York

STEVEN KEUCHER - Indiana University; Bloomington, Indiana

JAMES KLAIN - University of California, Los Angeles

RICHARD LANIER - Asian Cultural Council; New York

ERIC LARRABEE - New York

FRANK LATOURETTE - University of California, Los Angeles

HENRY LIN - The Ohio University; Athens, Ohio

W. MCNEIL LOWRY - Lowry Ltd.; New York

MARGARET LYNN - American Theater Association; Washington D.C.

MYRA MAYMAN - Radcliffe College and Harvard University; Cambridge, Massachusetts

ELIZABETH MCCORMACK - The Rockefeller Brothers' Fund; New York

EARL MCCUTCHEON - University of Georgia; Athens, Georgia

DONALD MCRAE - University of New Mexico; Albuquerque, New Mexico

KEITH MICHAELS - Indiana University; Bloomington, Indiana

AKRAM MIDANI - Carnegie-Mellon University; Pittsburgh, Pennsylvania

MICHAEL MILLER - New York University; New York

HOBE MORRISON - Variety; New York

MARY ANNE MORRISON - Athens, Ohio

DAVID OPPENHEIM - New York University; New York

JACK PELTASON - American Council on Education; Washington D.C.

JOE PRINCE - National Endowment for the Arts; Washington D.C.

T.C. RAYMOND - Harvard School of Business Administration; Cambridge, Massachusetts

CHARLES REINHARDT - American Dance Festival

DOLLYE ROBINSON - Jackson State University; Jackson, Mississippi

DAVID ROCKEFELLER, JR. - Arts, Education and Americans; Cambridge, Massachusetts

MR. AND MRS. JOHN SAVAGE; Vienna, Virginia

DAVID SCHNABEL - Pasadena City College; Pasadena, California

CAROL SCOTHORN - University of California, Los Angeles

HUGH SOUTHERN - National Endowment for the Arts; Washington D.C.

AUGUST STAUB - University of Georgia; Athens, Georgia

ROGER STEVENS - J.F. Kennedy Center for the Performing Arts;
Washington D.C.

MICHAEL STRAIGHT - Bethesda, Maryland

JOHN STRAUS - Consultant; New York

WILLIAM STULL - Ohio State University; Columbus, Ohio

RICHARD TEITZ - Dartmouth College; Hanover, New Hampshire

RALPH VERRASTRO - University of Georgia; Athens, Georgia

CHRYSTAL WATSON - Pasadena City College; Pasadena, California

ED WHALEN - Indiana University; Bloomington, Indiana

HENRY A. WICKE, JR. - Collegiate Institute; New York

MICHAEL WILSON - Pasadena City College; Pasadena, California

SHIRLEY WILSON - University of California, Los Angeles

SHIRLEY WIMMER - The Ohio University; Athens, Ohio

ABE WOLLOCH - University of California, Los Angeles

APPENDIX B

PROFILES OF SELECTED COLLEGES AND UNIVERSITIES

AUTHOR'S NOTE

Profiles of the seventeen institutions in the 1973 study have been updated and are presented here (see note 21). They are designed to inform the reader of some current trends and conditions of the arts on each campus. Readers are referred to Appendix F for the complete text of the questionnaire.

A scan of these profiles reveals the direct, current involvement in the campus mix. In discussions with officials on each of the campuses, there was overall agreement that the arts were being treated no better or worse than the other areas. Two of the campuses were reported as being treated better than most. Two other campuses where the arts are in trouble are historically black institutions in general financial disarray. What does not come out in the profiles and the interviews is the erosion of quality due to the economic crunch. There is an uneasy awareness of the perceived or actual damage, but, other than losing new appointments, there is no perceived deterioration in quality. Such a perception may be whistling in the dark out of loyalty to the institutions.

Notes

21   Morrison, 1973. (See Chapter 4 for a comparison of original profile data.)

ANTIOCH COLLEGE
(Washington-Baltimore Campus)

This institution no longer exists--although outcomes of its efforts remain in the Washington-Baltimore area.

Current administrators agree that the major reason for the demise was financial. There were other forces at work. A detailed case study of this important effort could be useful. It is likely that such a study would reveal a conflict in academic and managerial style with major differences between those of a social science orientation and those of an arts orientation.

The Washington-Baltimore campus of Antioch was one of the "experimental colleges" of the period and the findings from that experiment could be extremely useful in further dialogue on post-secondary administrative policy for the future of the arts on campus.

BENNINGTON COLLEGE

Progress for Bennington has been that of staying alive--
survival, with its basic premise of integrating the liberal
arts with the visual and performing arts in this difficult
time. This progress is marked by a dynamic "steady-state."

But financial problems are nothing new at Bennington. It
was founded in the late 20s and developed in the midst of
depression. That a $6 million Visual and Performing Arts
Center was opened in 1976 attests to the dynamics of this
steady state during the last decade (see Figure 2). The
faculty and the administration are meeting their problems with
vigor. In fact, a "reverse lend-lease idea," using the campus
acreage as leverage for fund-raising, was introduced by
Bennington. With the alumni and a "little bit of luck,"
Bennington, as one of the better known "experimental
colleges," keeps the idea and fact of integrating the arts
with the liberal arts alive and flourishing in our society.
Interdisciplinary majors and double-majors abound. It's
encouraging that students who have the need for such
"Bennington Integration" have a place to go.

FIGURE 2. Aerial view of Bennington College with Arts Center in foreground: (a) Lester Martin Drama Workshop, (b) Martha Hill Dance Workshop, (c) Susan A. Greenwall Music Workshop. (photo by Alex Brown).

BENNINGTON COLLEGE

Administration

No basic change

Bennington College continues its basic curricular approach as continuing the arts with liberal art studies. As a former Dean said, "Bennington does not have a curriculum, it has a faculty." There are no departments. The "head" of each unit is called a "Faculty Secretary."

Student Personnel

Little change, if any. The student body continues to be about 600. In the Fall of 1982, the enrollment was 642; in Fall of 1983, 637.

Faculty Personnel

Faculty in the arts is about the same. There are 33 FTE in the arts out of a faculty of 70. This is 14 more than reported ten years ago.

Budget: 1982-83

No change in dollars--ignoring inflation.

Space & Equipment

In 1976, a new $6,000,000 Visual and Performing Arts Center was added providing much needed space and equipment. Reports are that the Center is highly effective and a testament to Bennington's continuing commitment to the arts.

Scholarships

No response

Qualitative Considerations

No change

Arts Events

No change

CARNEGIE-MELLON UNIVERSITY

Along with the rest of the University, the College of Fine
Arts is embarked on a mission which is at once challenging and
promising as well as hazardous and baffling. The University,
in all of its departments, is seeking a common denominator
with the concept of decision-making. That is, the basic
function in any venture, engineering or the arts, comes down
to a critical moment in which a decision is made by someone.

In the meantime, the College and its departments are
forging ahead. There is good administrative support: witness
the new theater building (see Figure 3). How well all of
these developments are affecting the recruiting of students is
a question. There is a question, too, as to how well there is
a "fit" between some arts (rather than others) with the
concept of decision-making as a basic function. There is
little doubt that Carnegie-Mellon University will continue to
be a strong force in the arts in higher education.

FIGURE 3. College of Fine Arts Building, Carnegie-Mellon University.

130

CARNEGIE-MELLON UNIVERSITY

Administrative

No change

Student Personnel

Number of Majors in the Arts in 1982

Undergraduate	1982	1981	1982
Architecture	254	265	278
Music	121	129	128
Theater	188	181	185
Art	238	245	233
Design	183	165	164
TOTAL	984	985	988

Graduate			
Architecture	73	65	69
Music	25	26	40
Theater	36	36	43
Art	11	12	6
Design	0	1	1
TOTAL	145	140	159

Note: Quotes have been set as optimal enrollments in each art. Actual enrollments are slightly on the down side. Enrollment may be affected on the up side by introducing "minors" in the arts in the very near future.

Faculty Personnel (1982-83)

	Number of Full-time Faculty (FTE)	Number of Part-time Faculty (Bodies)	Number of Students Teaching Assts.
Architecture	18	17	8
Music	12	40	1
Theater	13	6	0
Art	19	4	2
Design	11	6	0

Budget: 1982-83

		% for salaries	
Architecture	- 1,052,673	76.3	81.7% budget goes for salaries
Music	- 888,893	90.2	18.3% " " for operating exp.
Theater	- 959,279	80.3	
Art	- 821,313	89.4	Total college budget-$4,607,880
Design	- 301,797	-	
Other	- 383,925	55.3	

Note: The arts are faring about the same as other departments on campus under the current budget crunch.

Space and Equipment

1. Capital investment in buildings--not answered
2. Total number of square feet (other than classrooms)

         Architecture - 37,506
         Music   - 16,950
         Theater   - 46,236
         Art   - 57,911
         Design   - 25,256
         Other   -   4,035
            TOTAL   186,979

   All departments have prospered appreciably as far as space is concerned, but it is reported that the present plant is not adequate.

3. Renovation at the cost of $500,000 is needed.

4. Capital investment for special equipment.

         Architecture - 24,884
         Music   -   9,875
         Theater   - 11,325
         Art   - 18,340
         Other   - 10,466

5. Not answered

Scholarships

	Number of undergrad scholarships	Total amt in $'s	Number of graduate scholarships	Total amt in $'s
Architecture	3	$ 8,000	10	$71,000
Music	43	35,000	17	37,990
Theater	-	-	38	87,969
Art	13	61,000	-	-
Design	5	3,000	-	-

Qualitative Considerations

1a. Is creative work considered equivalent to research? Yes
1b. Advanced academic degree required? Yes
2.   Question of efficacy of tenure? Yes
3.   Effectiveness in following areas is felt to be:
     a) Contribution of new works? Moderate
     b) Development of new works? Moderate
     c) Development of increasingly sophisticated audience?
        Very effective
     d) Exploring contemporary trends? Very effective
     e) Exploration of heritage? Very effective
     f) Seeking new relationships? Moderate
4.   Effectiveness on schools? Emphasis is professional
     training, not arts education.
5.   Admission to undergraduate work: a) University admission
     requirements and b) Auditions and/or portfolio
6.   Student may be dropped: because of grades
7.   Impact on community: Medium
8.   Satisfied with contribution to field of working artists?
     Student - yes; Faculty - no

Arts Events

1.   Provision for funds above box office: no box office
2.   Are the arts directly involved in cultural events
     presented by off-campus artists? No
3.   N/A
4.

	Student/Faculty % of Audience	Community % of Audience
Architecture	90%	10%
Music	60	40
Theater	40	60
Art	90	10
Design	N/A	N/A

DARTMOUTH COLLEGE

In its way, Dartmouth continues to support its arts program very well. In the 1973-83 interim, it has increased faculty in the arts as well as the budget. A new gallery for modern works is in construction (see Figures 4 and 5). Hopkins Center is teeming with activity--a condition it was designed to foster. Film continues to be a popular force in the arts on campus. I heard one complaint. "The students aren't daring enough." Dartmouth may be a prototype for a "co-curricular" program in the arts; that is, there are academic departments, but the campus-wide action is across the student body. In many ways, it is not surprising that one of the fresh forces in modern dance is the Pilobulus company, invented by Dartmouth students. None of the students who created the company and its approach were "dance majors," but they had taken some courses in dance. Dartmouth has developed its own way of developing the arts on the Hanover campus.

FIGURE 4. Hopkins Center, Dartmouth College. (Photo by Stuart Bratesman.)

135

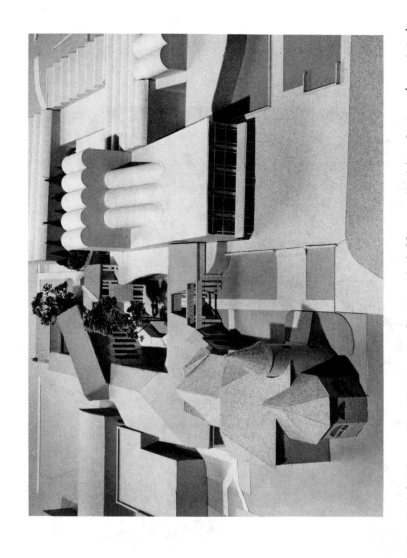

FIGURE 5. Model of new Hood Museum at Dartmouth College. Hopkins Center (on right) connects to Museum by arched passageway in center of photo. (Photo by Stuart Bratesman.)

DARTMOUTH COLLEGE

Administration

same

Student Personnel

about the same--"up a bit"

Faculty Personnel

Number of full-time faculty	1982-83	1970-71
Music	9	7.8
Theater	9.5	7
Visual Arts*	6	10

* It is contemplated that the Department of Art will become two autonomous departments: Art History and Visual Studies.

Budget: 1970-71

"Nothing is being cut." '83 budget will be greater than '82.

Space and Equipment

A new gallery for modern works is in construction. Hopkins Center is fully operational.

Scholarships

No change

Qualitative Considerations

Essentially the same, although tenure is not considered as a "growing question."

Arts Events

Although no details are given for 1982-83, the impact of arts events on students, faculty and surrounding commodity is reported as being "strong."

DUKE UNIVERSITY

There is ferment on the Duke campus in the arts area, something like Dartmouth's approach. But Duke has an indigenous quality that bodes well. The thought comes from the three-year old Institute of the Arts and its director, Professor James Applewhite, a poet in the English department. Whatever the ultimate shape the Institute takes, Duke will not be the same. With good administrative support, the arts are now a vital and growing force in the academic scene. The 80s promise to be the decade of the arts for Duke. In any case, it will be a campus well worth watching. The auspices are particulary good.

DUKE UNIVERSITY

Administration

3. A major change in Duke's Administration of the arts occurred with the initiation of The Institute of the Arts in 1981. The Institute "-coordinates activities in the performing and creative arts, thus encouraging the interrelationship of programs in dance, drama, film, imaginative writing, musical performance and composition, and studio art. All performing and creative artists are Fellows of the Institute, whether regular faculty members or distinguished artists in residence. The Institute assembles representatives of the various artistic disciplines into a single body for the planning of inter-disciplinary courses, yearly themes, and special events. Courses and festivals sponsored by the Institute bring together different art forms, integrating aesthetic appreciation with historical study and critical analysis. Student awards, honors projects, performances and exhibitions are sponsored." The following departments (or programs) are currently operating:

```
Dance (Program within Institute of the Arts)
Film  (    "              "              " )
Music
Theater (Program within Institute of the Arts)
Writing (    "              "              "
          and concentration within English
          Department)
Visual Arts
```

4. Tradition and planning

Student Personnel

1. Number of majors enrolled in the arts:

82-83	81-82	79-80	'71	'70
43	37	30	40	35

2. Total number of all students in fall term*:

	1982	1981	1980	1971	1970
Dance	159	181	180	224	126
Film/TV	185	125	78	-0-	-0-
Music	635	638	777	392	420

Theater	138	143	127	-0-	-0-
Writing	44	59	60	-0-	-0-
Visual Arts	123	123	159	301	382

* The noticeable difference in the number of students and their distribution is due, of course, to the introduction of "The Institute of the Arts" in 1981. These numbers represent a major change in University policy and administration. Enrollment for majors is up; for class enrollments it is the same.

Faculty Personnel

	Full-time	Part-time
Dance	1	3
Film/TV	1	11*
Music	13	22
Theater	1	4 (9*)
Writing	4	-
Visual Arts	2	7

* Faculty from other departments

Budget	1982-1983	1970-1971
Dance	$ 63,849	$ 23,462
Film	25,896	-0-
Music	788,438	216,881
Theater	78,153	-0-
Writing	143,768	-0-
Visual Arts (including Design Division)	118,934	NR
Institute of the Arts	40,633	-0-
Museum of Art	99,699	-0-
TOTAL	$1,359,370	NR

* Salaries of writers in English department

Space and Equipment

1. N/A
2. Space for specialized studio & lab in square feet.

Dance	4,915
Music	6,439

Theater	5,326
Visual Arts	4,910
Museum	11,697

3. Space is inadequate for the program.
4. N/A
5. N/A

Scholarships

Approximately 7 in music for total of $15,000
Work-study funds--$33,000

Qualitative Considerations

1a. Criteria for promotion currently in debate.
 b. Same
2. Yes (as anticipated)
3a. (New works) -Yes
 b. Moderate effect on audience
 c.   "   "
 d.   "   "
 e.   "   "
4. Some desire notes
5. University in consultation with department
6. May be dropped due to grades
7. Strong impact
8. Not satisfied although significant artists have been contributed

Arts Events

1. Yes. 66,000
2. Yes. Narrative description of Institute
3. 63
4. Percentage of audience as:

	Student-Faculty	Community
Dance	50%	50%
Film	65	35
Music	50	50
Theater	50	50
Writing	75	25
Visual Arts	65	35

EARLHAM COLLEGE

There is little change in the arts on the Earlham campus. Earlham continues to be an exemplary small liberal arts campus in a dynamic steady-state. Nowhere are the arts more central to the main effort--the well-rounded undergraduate education known as "liberal arts." The faculty is not only concerned with their careers and their departments, but their college as a whole. Therefore, the arts share equally on college matters such as budgets and faculty FTE's. What a major research university would seldom tolerate--double and triple majors-- Earlham does very well because their focus is on the individual in his/her undergraduate work. For the multi-talented student, Earlham may be the most productive preparation for graduate work in the arts. The one sour note I heard at Earlham was faculty overload in order to balance the budget. The faculty understands the problem, the pressures and go along with this solution. But mentally and physically, they may not be able to carry it much longer.

EARLHAM COLLEGE

Administration

2. Steady-state
3.   "
4.   "

Student Personnel

Number of majors enrolled in the arts*:

	Fall			
	1982	1981	1980	1971
Music	6	6	6	2
Theater (Speech/Drama)	6	6	6	N/A
Visual Arts	18	18	18	4

* The numbers are "marginally educated guesses." In comparison to 1971, for example, it is only fair to say "more" rather than a specific number. There are a number of "interdepartmental majors" which do not show here.

2. Class enrollments are about the same.

Faculty Personnel

	Number of Full-time Faculty	Part-time	Sum of all FTE's
Dance	-	1/4	1/4
Film	-	1/6	1/6
TV	-	1/6	1/6
Film/TV	-	1/6	1/6
Music	2	8	4
Theater	-	-	2
Visual Arts	2	4	3.5

Budget: 1982-83

N/R
The arts are holding their own in budget matters

Space and Equipment

1. About the same
2. About the same
3. OK
4. N/A
5. N/A

Scholarships

6 in music

Qualitative Considerations

1a. About the same
 b. "   "
2. N/R
3. But not effective enough
4-6. N/R
7. OK but never "satisfied"
8. "   "

Arts Events

1. No
2a. N/A
 b. N/A
3. N/A

FISK UNIVERSITY

Presently, as the concerned lay public knows from the media, Fisk is deep in financial problems of catastrophic proportion. The arts in this situation are as vulnerable as any other curricular area, but they are not singled out for disproportionate cuts. If Fisk survives, the arts will survive. What concerns teacher-administrators in the arts at Fisk is that the present stampede towards technology will leave the humanities and the arts virtually wiped out. Many at Fisk are proud of their record as a university committed to the liberal arts and their record in providing a sound undergraduate education for a historically black campus. Whatever the outcome of the current problem may be, those in the arts expect to be in the middle of it.

FISK UNIVERSITY

Administration

    1a. Dance
          Music
          Theater
          Visual Arts
    2-4. About the same

Division of Humanities and Fine Arts established in 1976

Staff Personnel

(Total rise in enrollment is down)
1. Number of majors enrolled - N/A
2. Total class enrollments, major & non-major
    undergraduate:

	1983	1971
Dance	42	95
Music	131	450
Theater (Drama/Speech)	241	300
Writing	5	20
Visual Arts	75	450
Creative Arts*	120	-

* Interdisciplinary (art, music, literature)

Faculty Personnel

	1973	Part-time	Sum of FTE	(1972)
Dance	1	-	1	1
Music	6	-	6	10
Theater (Drama/ Speech)	4	1	5	N/A
Writing	¼	-	¼	1
Visual Arts	3	-	3	5
Creative Arts	N/A	-	N/A	N/A

Budget:	1982-83	1970-71
Dance	$ 16,325	$ 13,000
Film	-	3,000
Music	162,938	120,000
Theater	81,421	50,000
Writing	-	5,000

Visual Arts   83,308   85,000

    TOTAL 1982-83 Budget: $344,032

Note: Administrators report that the arts are suffering budget cuts no worse than the university as a whole.

Scholarships

    N/A

Space and Equipment

    1. About the same. Art gallery is being renovated.
    2. Square feet studio space
    3-4. About the same. Space is inadequate. A Fine Arts Center is needed. Equipment needed:

Dance	100,000
Theater	500,000
Music	350,000
Visual Arts	50,000

Qualitative Considerations

    1a. Yes
    b. Yes (a change)
    2. No
    3a. Moderate plus
    b. "   "
    c. "   "
    d. Very effective
    e. "   "
    4a. Moderate plus
    5. University admissions without recourse to department
    6. Same
    7. N/A
    8. Strong
    9. Same-no

Arts Events

    1. N/A
    2a. Yes
    b. Yes
    3. Same

4.

	Student/Faculty	Community
Dance	80%	20%
Film	90	10
Music	80	20
Theater	98	2
Visual Arts	50	50

HARVARD UNIVERSITY

The arts at Harvard are still basically extra-curricular
--although some new courses in the arts have been added in the
last few years. The Office for the Arts, whose head reports
to the president of Harvard and the president of Radcliffe,
offers a "Learning from Performers Program," which may be the
most effective way of increasing undergraduate experience in
the arts in the country. The support from the administration
increases and the faculty is more inclined to consider the
arts as useful to undergraduate education. What Harvard does
with the next decade will be interesting to see. At present
it appears that Harvard can develop predominantly along one of
these paths: extra-curricular, co-curricular, or curricular.
Time and the vagaries of academic policy will tell.

HARVARD UNIVERSITY

Administration

In the last decade, under President Bok, three concrete steps have been taken altering the administration of the arts in a substantial way; according to a Harvard College administrator:
1) Creation of the Office for the Arts with its Learning from Peformers Programs*
2) The adoption by the faculty of guidelines for instruction that include performance credits--the expression of this endorsement in core curricular courses.
3) The invitation to the American Repertory Theater Company under Robert Brustein, to come to Harvard--the approval of drama courses for credit.
All of these steps were taken with the full support of faculty, students and alumni.

* Under the direction of Myra Mayman

Student Personnel

1. N/A
2. N/A

Faculty Personnel: 1982-83

	Full-time Sr. Faculty	Full-time Jr. Faculty	Student Teaching Assistants
Music	8.16	5.0	7.20
Theater	English Dept.	-	-
Writing	1.00	9.45	3.61
Visual Arts	8.97	7.20	5.51
Fine Arts	7.23	6.25	4.00

Budget: 1982-83

Music	$ 818,000
Theater	300,000
Writing	547,000
Visual Studies	1,250,000
Other	104,000
Fine Arts	512,000

TOTAL college budget $ 23,831,000

Space and Equipment

1. N/R
2-5. N/A

Scholarships

N/A
(Scholarships are awarded on the basis of need).

Qualitative Considerations

1a. No
 b. No (most have the Ph.D.)
2. No
3a. effective
 b. very effective
 c. effective
 d. very effective
 e. very effective
4. Yes
5. By the college
6. Grades
7. Graduate college
8. Medium to strong
9. Moderately

Arts Events

1. Yes
2. No
3. N/A

INDIANA UNIVERSITY

Indiana University is one of the major research universities
which does not operate its arts program with a College of Fine
Arts. Asked why he didn't appoint a Dean for Fine Arts when
he was President at Bloomington, Herman Wells said, "I looked
for one, but I didn't find one I wanted." In any case, the
arts continue to get strong administrative support, but the
support is uneven and the arts departments don't see much of
each other. There is some talk about the need for a single
administrative unit for the arts. The significance of the
arts to the community of Bloomington and surrounding areas
continues to be great. Indiana may be edging up to some kind
of metamorphosis in administration of the arts. As a major
research university, its development will be significant to
other campuses of a similar nature.

INDIANA UNIVERSITY

Administration

2. Departments in the Arts--1982-83

   Dance (included with the School of Music)
   TV
   Music
   Theater
   Writing
   Visual Arts

3. -
4. Same (Dept. of Theater and Drama separated from Dept. of Speech Communications. MFA in Creative Writing was added.)

Student Personnel

1. Number of Majors

	Undergraduate			Graduate
	1982	1981	1980	1982
Dance	(included in Music)			
TV	907	751	684	40
Music	1,010	1,030	1,035	661
Theater	174	216	264	69
Writing	(no undergraduate majors)			
Visual Arts	365	383	417	137

   TOTAL in the Arts: 3,393

2. Total Number of Class Enrollments: 1982-83

		Graduate	
	1982	1981	1980
Dance	(with music)		
TV	106	80	34
Music	1,892	1,933	1,853
Theater	182	161	161
Writing	80	60	40
Visual Arts	137	140	153

Note: Indiana has set enrollment limits and keeps them.

| | Undergraduate | | |
	1982	1981	1980
Dance	(with music)		
TV	2,058	1,718	1,589
Music	7,914	8,356	8,816
Theater	685	681	737
Writing	460	450	440
Visual Arts	2,200	2,338	2,513

Faculty Personnel

	Number of Full-time	Number of Part-time	Sum of FTE's	Student TA's
Dance	(with music)			
TV	16	10	18	16
Music	140	4	142	265
Theater	19	1	19.5	11
Writing	5	-0-	5	12
Visual Arts	33	2	35	42

Budget: 1982-83

	Dollar amt.	% Salaries	% Operating Exp.
Dance	(with music)		
TV	$ 730,000	85	16
Music	8,200,000	90	10
Theater	640,000	97	3
Writing	180,000	95	5
Visual Arts	1,440,000	90	10

Space and Equipment

1. 74,200,000
2. Number of square feet of studio space
   Dance - (with music)
   TV   - 7,257
   Music   - 77,948
   Theater   - 10,988
   Visual Arts - 77,982
3a. Renovated square feet needed - 48,000
 b. Additional renovated square feet needed - 140,000
4. Capital investment for special equipment: $5,462,000
   Capital investment for special equipment for each
   department:

	Original cost	Replacement cost
Dance	375,000	554,000
TV	1,875,000	4,375,000
Music	29,000	55,000
Theater	17,000	26,000
Writing (entire English department)		
Visual Arts	228,000	452,000

5. N/A (TV needs 550,000)

Scholarships

	Number of Undergrad Scholarships	Total Amt. in dollars	Number of Graduate Scholarships	Total Amt. in dollars
Dance (with music)				
TV	7	$ 2,500	16*	$ 72,000
Music	200	175,000	17	25,100
Theater	1	500	1	1,000
Writing	1	500	25*	1,000
Visual Arts	8	800	10	27,000

* Scholarship money is combined with College of Arts & Sciences Assistantship Awards.

Qualitative Considerations

1a.	Yes
b.	Yes and No
2.	No
3a.	Very effective
b.	" "
c.	" "
d.	" "
e.	" "
4.	Yes
5.	A and C (depends on department)--University clears first
6.	Music may drop on basis of talent. All others on grades.
7.	By the College
8.	Strong
9.	Yes

Arts Events

1.   N/A
2a. Yes
 b. Yes
3.   N/A
4.   Student/Faculty %   Community

     Music   80   20
     Theater   80   20
     Visual Arts   95   5

JACKSON STATE UNIVERSITY

Jackson State University has come a long way in the last
decade and the arts have developed along with it.
Nonetheless, some of its administrators point out that,
relatively speaking, Jackson State is still "separate but not
equal." Unfortunately, class enrollments in the arts are
down. The arts are suffering, but, according to some of the
faculty, they are suffering no worse than the rest of the
University. The faculty feel as if the arts are an integral
part of the Jackson State academic scene, and that they are
getting their fair share of fiscal support (see Figure 6).
The University reflects the current state of a historically
black college on the brink of bankruptcy. Under these
circumstances, it is difficult for the arts, in company with
the rest of the campus, to bring the arts program up to
present University standards in the arts. The gains of the
last decade are real, but there is still a long way to go.
One of the symptoms of the current difficulty is the rapid
turnovers in administrative leadership. Some report that a
president's tenure is measured in months rather than years.
This makes it difficult to use what resources exist
effectively. Because the arts are the newest addition to the
curricular life of any university, backing from the president,
who knows and supports the arts, is vital to further progress.

FIGURE 6. Frederick D. Hall Music Center, Jackson State University.

JACKSON STATE UNIVERSITY

Administration

2. Departments:

    Music
    Film/TV - Department of Mass Communications
    Writing - (in the English department)
    Visual Arts

Student Personnel

1. Number of majors enrolled in the arts:
    1983: Art   - 42
          Music - 98

2. Total class enrollments:
    1983: Art   -   393
          Music - 1,484

The following are concentrations or minors and do not
have separate records: Drama, Dance, TV/Radio.

Enrollments are down for majors and class enrollments.

Budget: 1982-83

Art	$ 202,328
Music	494,849
Dance	N/A
Dramatic Art	N/A
Radio/TV	N/A

Space and Equipment

N/A

Scholarships

N/A

Qualitative Considerations

1a. Is creative work equivalent? Yes
 b. Advanced degree required? Yes
 2. Concern for tenure? N/A

3. Effectiveness:
    a. Consideration of new works - Moderate
    b. Sophistication of audiences - Very effective
    c. Contemporary trends - Moderate
    d. Exploration of heritage - Very effective
    e. New relationships in the arts - Very effective
4. Effect on K-12? Yes
5. Undergraduate admission - University requirements, consultation of department, plus audition or portfolios
6. Student may be dropped for - lack of talent and grades
7. Impact on community - medium
8. Contribution of "successful" working artists - Yes, Yes

Arts Events

1. Provided with funds? Yes
    Amount - N/A
2. Are the arts involved?
    a. by having ex officio members - Yes
    b. relating to curricular work - Yes
3. N/A
4. N/A

NEW YORK UNIVERSITY

The Tisch School of the Arts has emerged strongly from the
"crazy quilt" administrative structure which existed (and
still exists to some extent) at NYU some ten years ago. The
Tisch School concentrates on the development of artists while
other parts of the University tend to take care of scholarly
and educational concerns of the arts. The "crazy quilt"
pattern seems to work very well for NYU. One development is
the area of "Performance Studies," which doesn't profess to
turn out artists but does profess to pursue the nature of
performance with a mixture of anthropological, psychological
and artistic means. Shamans as well as dancers, gospel
singers and other performers are studied. One is reminded of
Peter Brooks' Theater research in Paris. There is a direct
concern with the audience, and their research may soon affect
concepts of "arts for the people" which have arisen in
elitist-egalitarian debates. In any case, NYU has capitalized
effectively on the existence of a "world-class" arts community
in New York. Certainly, the structure of the Tisch School of
the Arts at NYU could not exist anywhere else. Its
relationship to the city appears to be a true symbiosis.

NEW YORK UNIVERSITY

Administration

2. Dance
    Film (Graduate)
    Radio/Film/TV (Undergraduate)
    Theater
    Dramatic Writing
    Cinema Studies
    Performance Studies
    Interactive Communication
    Musical Theater
    Photography

Note: Growing separately from the Music program is Washington Square College, the Institute of the Arts and the Visual Arts, the School of the Arts (now the Tisch School of the Arts). The Tisch School of the Arts has focused on the challenge of turning out artists. History (except for cinema studies) and arts education is left in other hands. Performance studies reflect an anthropological approach. Among other things, this has effectively sharpened the approach to fund-raising which has been very productive under President John Brademas.

Student Personnel (Awaits Miller response)

1. Number of majors enrolled in the arts:
    Dance
    Film/TV
    Theater
    Dramatic Writing
    Interactive Television
    Musical Theater
    (Enrollment has been up over the last five years)
2. Total Class enrollment: 2,700
    Individual enrollment:
    Film/TV (undergraduate) - 1,010
    Film/TV (graduate)   -   140
    Drama (undergraduate)   -   600
    Musical theatre   -   16
    Dramatic writing   -   125
    Interactive Tele-
      Communications   -   160
    Performance studies   -   150
    Cinema   -   150

Acting/Directing	-	96
Design	-	105
Dance	-	116
Photo	-	60

Faculty Personnel: 1982-83

	Number of Full-time	Number of Part-time	Sum of FTE	Teaching Assistants
Cinema Studies	6	-	-	7
Dance	5	8	-	3
Photography	1	3	-	-
Performance Studies	5	2	-	15
Film/TV	17	70	-	53
Undergraduate Drama	4	-	-	7
Theater	15	15	-	20
Interactive TV	3	13	-	5
Musical Theater	-	5	-	2

Budget: 1982-83

(to be supplied)

Space and Equipment

1. N/A
2. N/A
3. N/A
4. N/A
5. N/A

Scholarships

	Number of Undergrad Scholar-ships	Total Amt. in $'s	Number of Graduate Scholar-ships	Total Amt. in $'s
Cinema Studies	25	$ 43,000	29	$ 40,000
Dance	33	58,000	9	18,000
Photography	23	37,000	-	-
Performance Studies	-	-	34	38,000
Film/TV	376	676,000	57	131,000
Undergraduate Drama	257	380,000	-	-

Theater (inc. Acting, Design, Directing)	37	63,000	72	157,000
Dramatic Writing	42	79,000	20	45,000
Intertelevision	-	-	18	32,000
Musical Theater	-	-	15	61,000

Qualitative Considerations

1a. Yes
 b. No
2. Yes
3a. Very effective
 b. N/A
 c. Very effective
 d.   "   "
 e. Moderate
4. N/A
5. By the school. Auditions and/or portfolio plus admission office.
6. Lack of talent
7. By the school
8. N/A
9. Yes - but not really satisfied.

Arts Events

1a. Yes
 b. N/A
2a. No
 b. No
3. N/A
4. N/A

PASADENA CITY COLLEGE

Community colleges in California and their shrinking budgets
and growing student fees are presently front page headlines in
the daily papers. The resulting uncertainty is disrupting all
the two-year colleges in the state. 100,000 fewer students
(state-wide) enrolled in the Fall of 1983 than the year
before. Less heralded but perhaps more dangerous is a shift
from local control of the community colleges to state
domination. All of these forces and others must considered
when looking at the state of the arts at Pasadena City College
today. The department heads in the arts feel that they are
fairing as well as can be expected under the circumstances.
There is no concern that the arts will be "wiped out." But
the number of faculty has been squeezed down.

The "economic crunch" appears to be hitting the 2-year
college in a more damaging way than the small 4-year liberal
arts college, the comprehensive university, or the major
research university. In fact, there seems to be a
hierarchical response to the "economical crunch" in American
education. The least hit to the worst hit goes from the major
research university to the comprehensive university, to the
4-year liberal arts college, the 2-year community college, the
high school, and finally the worst hit--the elementary school.
Pasadena City College fits into this hierarchy as an example
of what is happening in the state. With its long history of
supporting the arts, Pasadena, even in its serious condition,
may be better off than most of the 2-year colleges. That's
"good-bad news" at its most ambivalent. For good or ill, the
crunch is forcing decisions which may be very influential in
the arts program for the next ten or fifteen years.

PASADENA CITY COLLEGE

Administration

   2.   Architecture
       Film
       TV
       Music
       Theater
       Writing
       Visual Arts

Student Personnel

   1.   Number of Majors Enrolled in the Arts

	1982-83	1981-82	1980-81
Music	-	-	-
TV/Radio	140	160	75
Theater	75	75	75
Visual Arts - N/A	-	-	-

   2.   Total Number of Class Enrollments

	1982-83	1981-82	1980-81
Music - N/A	-	-	-
TV/Radio	700	600?	600?
Theater	600	600?	600?
Visual Arts	3,217	3,027	3,274

Faculty Personnel

	Number of Full-time	Number of Part-time	Sum of FTE's	Teaching Assts.
Music	7.74	1	8.81	3
TV/Radio	5	4-8	6-8	-
Theater	3	6-8	5.7	-
Visual Arts	N/A	-	-	-

Budget: 1982-83

Music	$ 635,000
TV/Radio	N/A
Theater	16,000-(Production funds)
Visual Arts	969,452-(72 1/3% for salaries)

Space and Equipment

Music   )
TV/Radio   ) N/A - (All are in serious need of more space and
Theater   )   equipment)
Visual Arts)

Scholarships

N/A

Qualitative Considerations

    1a. N/A
     b. Yes - a B.A. or B.F.A. - M.F.A. desirable
    2.   Yes
    3a. Moderately
     b. Not enough
     c.   "   "
     d.   "   "
     e. Moderately
    4.   No
    5.   By the college
    6.   May not be dropped
    7.   Medium
    8.   Not enough

Arts Events

    1.   Yes
    2a. No
     b. No
    3.   N/A
    4.   N/A

PENNSYLVANIA STATE UNIVERSITY

Pennsylvania State University continues to be a stabilizing force in the arts in higher education. The economic crunch has not spared Penn State, but the arts have fared as well or even better than some of the academic areas of the University. "Solid" is the word for Penn State.

In the last decade, the major in arts education has moved from the School of Education to the College of Fine Arts--a significant move. And the College is one of the few Colleges of Fine Arts still to include architecture. It has also been charged with the responsibilities of extra-departmental operations of the University Gallery and arts events from off-campus. The College has also served in a producers' capacity by producing arts events with off-campus talent. Penn State may be considered the university prototype as the entity encompassing all arts activities on campus: curricular and co-curricular.

PENNSYLVANIA STATE UNIVERSITY

Administration

2. Architecture
   Film   (Dept. of Theater Arts)
   Music   (School of Music)
   Theater   (Dept. of Theater & Film)
   Visual Arts   (School of Visual Arts)
   Others   (Dept. of Art History)
                 (Dept. of Landscape Architecture)

   (There is considerable dance instruction in the
   College of Health, Physical Education & Recreation)

3. There is one administrative unit. The College of
   Arts & Architecture.
4. Careful design

Student Personnel

1. Number of Majors Enrolled in College

Total Fall 1982	Total Fall 1981	Total Fall 1980
1,320	1,457	1,511

Undergraduates	Fall '82	Fall '81	Fall '80
Architecture	218	276	266
Film	42	35	34
Music	114	130	139
Theater	149	164	165
Visual Arts	371	418	456
Art History	27	47	26
General Arts	21	24	25
Landscape Archi-tecture	206	206	211

Graduates	Fall '82	Fall '81	Fall '80
Architecture	8	5	7
Film	-	-	-
Theater	49	44	49
Visual Arts	48	63	71
Art History	23	23	20
General Arts	-	-	-

Landscape Architecture	-	-	-
Music	44	42	42

2. Class Enrollments

	1982-83	1981-82	1980-81
Architecture	1,056	1,131	986
Film	892	-	-
Music	2,209	2,262	2,236
Theater	1,722	2,959*	2,637*
Visual Arts	1,537	1,446	1,526
Art History	571	645	639
Landscape Architecture	693	576	530

* Included Film

Faculty Personnel

	Number of Full-time	Number of Part-time	Sum of FTE's	Teaching Assts.
Architecture	18.0	-0-	18.0	4
Music	31.6	6	34.0	28
Theater/Film	24.6	1	25.6	13
Visual Arts	36.9	-0-	36.9	17
Art History	9.8	4	10.3	6
Landscape Architecture	10.0	-0-	10.0	-0-

Budget: 1982-83

Architecture	$ 576,626
Film	121,312
Music	1,031,459
Theater	765,028
Visual Arts	1,269,162
Art History	377,734
Landscape Architecture	383,079
Administrative Research	436,196
TOTAL (% of salaries: 92) (% of operating expenses: 8)	$ 4,960,596

Space and Equipment

1. Architecture   551,750
    Film   112,600
    Music   1,599,368
    Theater   1,624,712
    Visual Arts   3,644,261
    Art History   278,752
    Landscape Archi-
       tecture   474,963

    TOTAL $ 8,286,206

Arts Service Units

    Museum of Art   4,034,000
    Artists Series   40,000
    Auditorium   8,488,000

    TOTAL Arts Service Unit $12,562,000

2. Number of square feet for specialized studio & lab
    use:
    Architecture   27,474
    Film   3,000
    Music   25,237
    Theater   35,000
    Visual Arts   66,280
    Art History   500
    Landscape Architecture 15,201

    TOTAL   172,692

Arts series units & college administration

    Artists Series   4,211
    Museum of Art   21,395
    College Administration 6,542
    Auditoriums   138,622

    TOTAL Arts series   170,770

3a. Renovated square feet needed - 35,000
 b. Additional square feet needed - to be determined for
    3 areas

4.   Capital investment for special equipment

Architecture, Landscape Arch.	185,750
Film	25,350
Music	315,000
Theater	520,000
Visual Arts	317,728
Art History	75,000
TOTAL	1,438,828

Arts series units & college administration

Artists series	21,000
College administration	45,000
Museum of Art	2,812,000
Auditorium	194,000
TOTAL	3,072,000

5.   Needed equipment for optimum operation:

Architecture	17,600
Film	150,000
Theater	500,000
Visual Arts	70,200
Music	112,200
Other (computer equipment for all)	150,000
TOTAL	1,000,000

Arts service units

Auditorium	143,000
Museum	150,000
TOTAL	293,000

Scholarships

	Number of Undergrad Scholarships	Total Amt. in $'s	Number of Graduate Scholarships	Total Amt. in $'s
Architecture	4	$ 3,000	(Assistantship/ 12 terms)	$ 13,608
Music	30	17,000	77	89,964
Theater/Film	4	2,450	115	125,748
Visual Arts	5	3,050	73	70,275
Art History	-0-	-	49	42,966
Landscape Architecture	10	2,725	-0-	-
Dean office	-0-	-0-	7	6,048

Qualitative Considerations

    1a. Yes
     b. Appropriate terminal degrees or equivalent
    2. No
    3. Effectiveness
       a. Very effective
       b. Moderate
       c.   "
       d.   "
       e.   "
    4. Yes
    5. Usually over admissions but sometimes in the College. The College requires auditions and/or portfolios.
    6. Grades
    7. Auditions and portfolios plus Graduate College
    8. Strong
    9. No

Arts Events

    1. Arts Services--Yes; Academic Units--No
    2. Artists Series--128,000
       University Resident Theater--294,000
       a. Yes
       b. Yes

3. 32
Admissions from off-campus	61,670
Income from off-campus	474,238
Expense for off-campus	423,077

4. Estimates of Audience

	% Student/Faculty	% Community
Architecture	75	25
Film	65	35
Music	75	25
Theater	65	35
Visual Arts	80	20
Art History	80	20
Landscape Arch- tecture	80	20
Artists Series	60	40
Museum of Art	55	45

UNIVERSITY OF CALIFORNIA, LOS ANGELES

UCLA has grown into a major research university and the arts continue in the College of Fine Arts as an integral part of that growth (see Figures 7 and 8). Presently, the College is charged with bringing all arts activities into its jurisdiction, including the presentation of off-campus attractions. Too often these kinds of operations produce a local "Sol Hurok." Like the late impresario, but not with their own money, the directors develop a fine program at University expense which has less and less to do with the University. It's a difficult problem and the UCLA College of Fine Arts is in the midst of managing it.

On the academic side, the College has the problem of shifting gears from a "comprehensive university" focusing on undergraduate work to the masters level to that of a "major research university" focusing on graduate and professional work, the doctorate, the post-doctoral programs and extra-departmental efforts such as institutes. With the speed of growth the University and the surrounding community has experienced, the problems are not simple and time is in short supply. How UCLA deals with these matters may well prove to be a prototype for the arts in the modern major research university. The stakes are high.

FIGURE 7. Schoenberg Hall Music Building, University of California, Los Angeles.

176

FIGURE 8. Dickson Art Center at University of California, Los Angeles. Houses classrooms and offices of the art department as well as galleries which have housed major exhibitions.

177

UNIVERSITY OF CALIFORNIA, LOS ANGELES

Administration

2. Dance
   Music
   Theater Arts (MP/TV)
   Art, Design & Art History

   Architecture is in a separate professional school

3. Same
4. Same

Student Personnel

1. Number of Majors Enrolled in the Arts: 2,200

Undergraduates	1982	1981	1980
Art	666	720	668
Dance	82	87	82
Music	220	215	226
Theater Arts (including MP/TV)	520	522	489

Graduates	1982	1981	1980
Art	150	168	158
Dance	95	100	92
Music	99	84	100
Theater Arts (including MP/TV)	368	411	429

2. Total Number of Class Enrollments

Undergraduates	1982	1981	1980
Art	1,884	1,793	1,999
Dance	651	664	564
Music	3,316	2,725	3,050
Theater Arts (& MP/TV)	1,884	1,841	1,845

Graduates	1982	1981	1980
Art	333	356	368

Dance	383	464	410
Music	291	216	240
Theater Arts (& MP/TV)	1,031	922	1,009

(Optimal enrollment limits for majors have been established)

Faculty Personnel

	Number of Full-time	Number of Part-time	Sum of FTE's	Teaching Assts.
Art	43	23	50.74	57
Dance	13	13	18.77	21
Music	46	29	58.09	49
Theater Arts	48	10	51.19	30

Budget: 1982-83

Art	$2,250,080
Dance	905,989
Music	3,018,574
Theater Arts	3,918,572
TOTAL	$10,093,215*

*(82.81% for salaries)
(17.19% for operating expenses)

Space and Equipment

1a. Capital investment for all college buildings: 17,922,510 (capitalized 1981-82--actual cost plus improvements)
  b. Capital investment for departments:

Art	4,531,385
Dance	250,974
Music	6,798,010
Theater Arts	6,179,353
Dean's office	162,788

2. Square feet of space:

Art	45,746
Dance	8,920
Music	28,217

Theater Arts   49,709

3. Additional square feet needed:

Art   30,000
Dance   58,000
Music   15,000
Theater Arts   80,000
(& MP/TV & Archives)
Dean's office   2,000

4. Capital investment in special equipment: 1,150,000
   (150,000--permanent)
   (1,000,000--temporary)

Art   70,000
Dance   30,000
Music   100,000 (estimates)
Theater Arts   900,000

5. Needed equipment for optimal operation:

Art   300,000
Dance   50,000
Music   300,000
Theater Arts   5,350,000

Scholarships

	Number of Undergrad Scholar- ships	Total Amt. in $'s	Number of Graduate Scholar- ships	Total Amt. in $'s
Art	149	$143,200	140	$335,000
Dance	18	19,037	70	141,000
Music	48	47,720	60	165,000
Theater Arts	87	97,208	150	274,000

Qualitative Considerations

1a. Is creative work accepted for research & promotion?
    Yes
 b. Degree required? No
2. Question of value of tenure--N/A
3. Effectiveness of department faculty
   a. Very effective
   b. "   "

    c. "   "
    d. "   "
    e. N/A
4. Effect on K-12? No
5. Admission for undergraduates--paper screen plus
    admissions office
6. May be dropped--because of grades
7. Admission to graduate work
    --with audition/portfolio plus graduate college
    --screening process for those who don't audition/
      portfolio
8. Impact on surrounding community? Yes
9. Contribution of successful working artists
    Faculty--N/A
    Student--Yes

Arts Events

1. Funds to produce arts events--Yes
2. College and departments directly involved with
    off-campus arts events
    a. Yes
    b. Dance--Yes
       Music--Yes
       Theater--Yes
       Art, Design, Art History--Yes
    c. No--Department of Fine Arts Productions reports to
       Dean of CFA
3a. Strong
 b. Attendance % at on-campus events:

	% Student/Faculty	% Community
Art	25	75
Dance	25	75
Music	20	80
Theater Arts	25	75

UNIVERSITY OF CALIFORNIA, SANTA CRUZ

The experimental developments in the arts on the Santa Cruz campus of the University of California are still in the process of developing. Perhaps the co-curricular approach to the arts (a mix of extra-curricular and curricular) may emerge here in hybrid fashion of its own. Just as Harvard is pursuing its own version of the arts offerings on campus (both curricular and extra-curricular), Santa Cruz is in the midst of creating its own form (see Figure 9). While there is a strong surge back towards a departmental rather than the original cluster-college approach, the colleges still exist and the original thrust towards an individualized undergraduate education still has force. The economic crunch makes for additional pressure on developments, but it's clear that whatever the outcomes molding the shape of this experiment, the arts, one way or another, will be there. Faculty personnel and budgets have virtually doubled in the last ten years.

Notes

Note: Begun at the same time as Santa Cruz, the State University of New York at Purchase (SUNY-Purchase) was an "experimental" college but with the clear mandate to train artists as well as educate them. It was too new to be in the original (1973) study, but now, having survived the economic crunch and changes in administrative leadership, it is beginning to blossom and deserves a study of its own idiosyncratic self.

ENTRY TO NORTH COURTYARD

ENTRY TO SOUTH COURTYARD

FIGURE 9. The Elena Baskin Visual Arts facility on the University of California, Santa Cruz campus.

183

UNIVERSITY OF CALIFORNIA, SANTA CRUZ

Administration

    2. Music
        Theater (includes film and dance)
        Visual Arts

    3. The arts are now an independent "Division, splitting
        from Arts & Humanities"

Student Personnel

    1. Number of Majors enrolled in the Arts

Undergraduates	1982	1981	1980
Music	62	62	48
Theater	55	63	65
Visual Arts	62	73	70

Graduates	1982	1981	1980
Music	-	-	-
Theater	6	-	-
Visual Arts	11	11	10

    2. Class enrollments

	1982	1981	1980
Music	551	548	576
Theater	590	668	606
Visual Arts	685	713	634

Faculty Personnel

	Number of Full-time	Number of Part-time	Sum of FTE's	Teaching Assts.
Music	7.17	9	12.03	0.50
Theater	5.55	12	12.95	1.00
Visual Arts	10.67	11	16.87	2.50

Budget: 1982-83

Music	$ 544,512
Theater	557,271

Visual Arts   755,324

90% salaries
10% operating expenses

Space and Equipment

1. The capital investment in buildings is $ 4,436,692
   (Book value--not replacement value)
2. Number of square feet for specialized use:

Music	7,897
Theater	6,350
Dance	5,329
Film	2,226
Visual Arts	30,769

3. The present plant is minimally effective.
4. Capital investment in equipment is $ 57,500

Music	$ 12,000
Theater	15,000
Visual Arts	14,000
Other	16,500

5. Projected costs of needed equipment is $ 20,000

Music	$ 7,000
Theater	3,000
Visual Arts	10,000

Scholarships

Graduate scholarships only	Number	Amt. in $'s
Music	-	-
Theater	12	$ 29,000
Visual Arts	10	24,000

Qualitative Considerations

1a. Is creative work considered? No
 b. Is Ph.D. required? No
2. Question of tenure? Maybe
3. Effectiveness of faculty
   a. Contribution of new works--moderate
   b. Sophisticated laity--very effective
   c. Exploration of trends--very effective

    d. Exploration of heritage--very effective
    e. New relationships--not enough
4. Effect on K-12? No
5. Admission--University admission without recourse to college/university
6. May be dropped--failure to pass sufficient courses
7. Impact on community--medium
8. Satisfied with contribution of artists--Faculty: Yes
                                                Student: No

Arts Events

1. Provided with funds--Yes
2. Directly involved with off-campus--Yes
3. Total number of arts events--150

    Number admission events off-campus - 2,000
    Income for arts events   - 8,000
    Expense for arts events   - 40,000

UNIVERSITY OF GEORGIA

The arts at the University of Georgia continue to thrive in the Division of Fine Arts, but its budgets are in a college with twenty-two other departments. The department chairs would prefer the arts to be in a separate administrative structure for the arts. (It is felt that a spokesman in the Division of Fine Arts--a dean, for example, who only represented the arts--would represent them more effectively.) After the years of success, there is, nevertheless, a feeling among the arts administrators that some changes are due, that there is a leaven at work which will provide the arts with a new impetus, a fresh approach to their work, that the arts will be speaking for themselves somehow (see Figure 10). There is also more of a sense of outreach to the community and the rest of the state.

FIGURE 10. Fine Arts Building, University of Georgia.

UNIVERSITY OF GEORGIA

Administration

   2. Music
      Theater
      Visual Arts
   3. (These three departments are in an unbudgeted
      division)
   4. Special needs of the arts are diffused on a college
      of 22 departments; prefer a separate administrative
      structure.

Student Personnel

   1. Number of Majors Enrolled in the Arts:

Undergraduates	1982	1981	1980
Music	320	306	340
Theater	101	100	105
Visual Arts	679	721	652

Graduates	1982	1981	1980
Music	49	68	76
Theater	49	39	45
Visual Arts	69	82	93

   2. Class Enrollments

Undergraduates	1982	1981	1980
Music	941	909	885
Theater	975	1,000	1,050
Visual Arts	1,880	1,773	1,700

Graduates	1982	1981	1980
Music	67	65	71
Theater	150	150	146
Visual Arts	157	N/A	N/A

Faculty Personnel: 1982-83

	Number of Full-time	Number of Part-time	Sum of FTE's	Teaching Assts.
Music	50	3	53	20
Theater	15	28	31	27
Visual Arts	54	4	58	5

Budget: 1982-83

Music	$ 1,200,000
Theater	700,000
Visual Arts	1,900,000
TOTAL	$ 3,779,716

93.5% salaries
6.5% operating expenses

Space and Equipment

1. The capital investment - 10,160,000
2. Number of square feet - 194,000
3. Addition of square feet needed - 25,000
4. Capital investment for special equipment - N/A - but this is a priority item.
5. N/A - but is a priority item

Scholarships

	Number of Undergrad Scholarships	Total Amt. in $'s	Number of Graduate Scholarships	Total Amt. in $'s
Music	30	$ 21,000	20	$ 8,000
Theater	-0-	-0-	-0-	-0-
Visual Arts	3	2,500	10	45,000

Qualitative Considerations

1a. Is creative work considered equivalent? Yes
 b. Advanced degree required? Yes
2.   Growing question of tenure? No

3. Effectiveness of faculty:
   a. New works - Very effective
   b. Increasingly sophisticated audience - Moderate
   c. Exploration of contemporary trends - Very
      effective
   d. Exploration of heritage - Moderate
   e. New relationships - Moderate
4. Effect on K-12 - Yes
5. Admission of undergraduate: Varied - music & drama
   audition
6. Criteria for dropping - Grades
7. Admission to graduate work - Audition/portfolio and
   grad college
8. Impact on surrounding community - Medium
9. Satisfied with contribution to "successful" artists?
   Faculty - Yes
   Student - Yes

Arts Events

1. Are you provided with funds? Yes
2. Are departments involved with off-campus events &
   artists?
   a. By having rep on committee - Yes
   b. Related to curricular work? Theater, Music &
      Visual Arts are not
3. Total number of arts events
   10 in Theater
   Total admissions - N/A
   Total income   - "
   Total expense   - "
4. Estimate of audience breakdown:

	% Student/Faculty	% Community
Music	50	50
Theater	60	40
Visual Arts	50	50

UNIVERSITY OF NEW MEXICO

The arts at the University of New Mexico are probably more in balance with the academic, spatial and fiscal nature of the campus than most. Although enrollments are off slightly, the economic crunch is not likely to do serious damage to the College of Fine Arts and it is being treated fairly by the University administration. Conditions are no better and no worse than the rest of the campus. The administrative structure is sound and the departments' goals accent a virile approach to teaching and research. They are a relatively snug operation which supports creative work in the making of art. If there are two main thrusts to the arts in higher education: (a) making art and (b) encountering art, the College of Fine Arts of the University of New Mexico elects to pursue the making of the arts.

UNIVERSITY OF NEW MEXICO

Administration

2. Music
    Theater (includes Dance, Film & TV)
    Visual Arts
    Tamarind Institute
3. Architecture became a School of Architecture
4. Assistant/Associate Chairs have been added

Student Personnel

1. Number of Majors Enrolled in the Arts

Undergraduates	1982	1981	1980
Dance	15	10	15
Music	108	119	149
Theater	59	54	52
Visual Arts	208	227	236

Graduates	1982	1981	1980
Dance	N/A	N/A	N/A
Music	30	33	37
Theater	16	7	8
Visual Arts	99	117	121

2. Class Enrollments

	1982	1981	1980
Dance	439	487	383
Film	137	100	220
Music	2,664	2,673	2,828
Theater	631	642	582
Visual Arts	1,933	2,089	2,326

Faculty Personnel

	Number of Full-time	Number of Part-time	Sum of FTE's	Teaching Assts.
Dance	4	3	6.5	-
Film	1	-	1	1
TV	1	-	1	-

Music	25	4	27	12
Theater	12	-	12	5
Visual Arts	28	14	32	39
Contingency	-	3	-	1

Budget: 1982-83

Dance	$ 106,800
Music	790,100
Theater (includes Film/TV)	385,500
Visual Arts	1,034,900
Tamarind	82,200
Non Department	40,000
TOTAL	**$ 2,892,900**

Space and Equipment

1. The capital investment for buildings is:

Music	$ 2,733,000
Theater (includes Dance, Film, TV)	2,360,000
Visual Arts	3,520,000
Art Museum	53,900

2a. Number of square feet - total is 133,800 square feet
  b. Music - 110,000
     Theater - 32,600 (includes Dance, Film & TV)
     Visual Arts - 109,250
     Art Museum - 14,600
     Concert Hall - 71,558
     Fine Arts Library - 10,850
     Tamarind Int. - 6,400

3. Present plant effective? Yes
    Need: 10,000 square feet renovated
          13,000 additional square feet

4. Investment in special equipment
Music	- 455,800
Theater (Dance, Film, TV)	- 136,900
Visual Arts	- 174,700

5. N/A

Scholarships

	Number of Undergrad Scholarships	Total Amt. in $'s	Number of Graduate Scholarships	Total Amt. in $'s
Dance	1	$ 50	-	-
Music	39	35,325	6	$ 29,700
Theater	8	4,525	1.5	7,425
Visual Arts	10	3,550	17	86,900
Other	-	-	1.33	8,170

Qualitative Considerations

1a. Creative work accepted? Yes
 b. Advanced degree required? At least masters
2. Question about tenure? No
3. Effectiveness of faculty:
   a. Contribute to new works - Very effective
   b. Increase of sophistication of audience - Moderate
   c. Explore contemporary trends - Very effective
   d. Explore heritage - Very effective
   e. N/A
4. Effect on K-12? Yes
5. Undergraduate admission - By the College after admission to the University
6. Student may be dropped - Because of grades
7. Graduate admission - Audition/portfolio by College plus Graduate College
8. Impact on community - Medium
9. Satisfied with successful working artists?
   Faculty - Yes
   Students - Yes

Arts Events

1. Are you provided with funds? Yes
2. Is the College or department involved?
   a. No
   b. No
   (Note: Departments mount their own)
3. Total number of arts events from off-campus: 5-8
   Total income: $ 15,427; Total admissions: 4,715;
   Total expense - N/A

4. Breakdown of audience:

	% Faculty-Student	% Community
Dance	66	33
Film	90	10
Music	75	25
Theater	66	33
Visual Arts	60	40

APPENDIX C

SCATTERGRAM

(Resistance/Support Ratings from Reporting Institutions)

RESISTANCE OR SUPPORT RATINGS FROM REPORTING INSTITUTIONS

SUPPORT	Local community	State Legislature	Federal agencies	Private state and local foundations	Private national foundations	Corporations	Business and merchants	Arts organizations	Idiosyncratic nature of artists & teachers	Collegiality of faculty
+ 5	o o o o							o	o	o o
+ 4	o	o o	o o	o o	o o	o	o o	o		o o o
+ 3	o o o o o		o o o	o o o	o o	o o	o o	o o		o
+ 2	o o	o	o o	o o o	o	o	o o o	o o	o o	o o
+ 1		o	o o o o	o o o	o o	o o o	o	o	o	o o
0	o	o o o o o o	o	o o	o o o o o	o o o o o	o o o o	o o o o	o o o o	
- 1		o o o	o							
- 2										
- 3										
- 4										
- 5										

RESISTANCE

N/A								o	o o o	o

RESISTANCE OR SUPPORT RATINGS FROM REPORTING INSTITUTIONS

SUPPORT	Social sciences disciplines	Science and math disciplines	Engineering and technology	Professional schools	School (college) of Education	Alumni association	Campus business office	Buildings and grounds	Alumni (general)	Alumni in the arts
+ 5	o				o	o o o	o o	o o	o o o	o o o o o
+ 4	o o	o o o	o	o o	o	o o	o	o	o	o o o
+ 3	o	o			o o o	o o		o	o o	o o o
+ 2	o o o	o		o	o	o o o	o o o o o	o	o	o
+ 1	o o	o o	o		o	o o		o	o o o	o
0	o o	o o o	o o o o o o	o o o o o o	o o	o	o o o o	o o o o o	o o o	
- 1	o		o							
- 2		o								
- 3										
- 4										
- 5										

RESISTANCE

	Social sciences disciplines	Science and math disciplines	Engineering and technology	Professional schools	School (college) of Education	Alumni association	Campus business office	Buildings and grounds	Alumni (general)	Alumni in the arts
N/A	o	o	o o o	o o o	o o		o	o		

RESISTANCE OR SUPPORT RATINGS FROM REPORTING INSTITUTIONS

SUPPORT	Board of Trustees	Chief executive	Chief officer of academic affairs	Vice-President of business affairs	Dean of the college in which arts reside	Academic senate	Student government	Student body at large	University curriculum council	Humanities disciplines
+ 5	oooo	ooooo	oooooo	oooo	oooooo	oo	oo	oo	ooo	oo
+ 4	oo	ooooo	oooo	o	oooo	ooo	oo	o	oo	oooo
+ 3		oo	ooo	ooo		oo	oo	ooooo	oooo	oooooo
+ 2	oo	o		oo			ooo	oo	o	o
+ 1	o		o	o		ooo		o	o	
0	oo			oo	oo	o	oooo	o	oo	
- 1		oo				o				o
- 2										
- 3										
- 4										
- 5										

RESISTANCE

N/A	oooo			o	o	o			o	

NOTE: BENNINGTON COLLEGE DID NOT RESPOND TO THIS PORTION OF THE SURVEY AND DUKE
UNIVERSITY ONLY ANSWERED THE FIRST HALF OF THIS CHART.

APPENDIX D

NATIONAL NORMS

Although the available national statistics describing the arts in higher education are spotty and will continue to be, unless the HEADS project is successful, some are given here as evidence that the arts are beginning to claim some attention nationally--and still have a long way to go.

Unfortunately, the work produced by Noah Meltz was not continued, and efforts to seek out new information on national norms was unrewarded.

It is believed that the statistical information reported here will be seen as first steps toward developing "institutional research" in the arts. There are many requests for such information but little or no funding for gathering it.

In short, up-to-date material is scarce or non-existent. The data provided here reflects a few shadows of the field but little more. The shadows, however, do give one pause to think.

THE GROWTH IN EARNED DEGREES IS PROJECTED AS FOLLOWS:

	1970-71 (Estimated)	1980-81 (Estimated)
Bachelor's and first professional	863,000	1,333,000
Natural sciences	188,860	257,200
Social sciences, humanitites	674,140	1,075,800
Fine arts	59,710	98,650
Master's	224,000	395,900
Natural sciences	44,060	70,860
Social sciences, humanities	179,940	325,040
Fine arts	14,210	25,060
Doctor's	32,000	68,700
Natural sciences	14,650	26,060
Social sciences, humanities	17,350	42,640
Fine arts	1,120	2,660

SOURCE: National Center for Educational Statistics (published in Chronicle of Higher Education, p. 1, April 17, 1972)

BACHELORS AND FIRST PROFESSIONAL DEGREES GRANTED IN THE UNITED STATES IN TOTAL NUMERICAL AND PERCENTAGE DISTRIBUTION FOR 1951, 1960, AND 1969

	Numerical distribution			Percentage distribution		
	1951	1960	1969	1951	1960	1969
Total graduations	386,266	391,194	769,222	100.00	100.00	100.00
Natural science and related				30.42	29.33	22.61
Agriculture, engineering, and forestry	53,638	45,163	52,456	13.89	11.55	6.82
Health professions	23,678	24,450	33,498	6.13	6.25	4.35
Science	40,155	45,090	88,036	10.40	11.53	11.44
Social sciences, humanities, and related				69.58	70.67	77.37
Architecture	2,644	1,801	3,477	0.68	0.46	0.45
Arts (Letters)	89,080	92,264	258,870	23.06	23.59	33.65
Education	65,038	71,145	121,669	16.84	18.19	15.82
Fine arts	9,890	12,887	35,024	2.56	3.29	4.55
Law	14,338	9,240	17,468	3.71	2.36	2.27
Music	7,723	7,593	12,107	2.00	1.94	1.57
Social work	2,951	2,498	8,404	0.76	0.64	1.09
Other	77,131	79,063	138,213	19.98	20.22	17.97

NOTE: Percentages may not add to 100 because of rounding.

SOURCE: Meltz, 1971a, p. 19

ALTERNATIVE PROJECTIONS OF THE DISTRIBUTION OF TOTAL BACHELOR'S GRADUATIONS BY FIELD OF STUDY
IN THE UNITED STATES IN 1981 AND ACTUAL DATA FOR 1961 AND 1969

| | Actual | | Estimated in 1981 | |
	1961	1969	A	B
Total graduations	397,383	769,222	1,170,080	1,170,080
Natural science and related				
Agriculture, engineering and forestry	42,431	52,456	73,480	59,680
Health professions	24,634	33,498	51,568	42,330
Science	46,563	88,036	130,184	140,310
Social sciences, humanities, and related				
Architecture	1,674	3,477	4,903	5,580
Arts (Letters)	97,645	258,870	396,940	529,535
Education	74,028	121,669	197,792	108,870
Fine arts	12,861	35,024	55,564	64,740
Law	9,429	17,468	24,620	23,780
Music	7,360	12,107	18,958	8,830
Social work	2,718	8,404	13,400	23,240
Other	78,040	138,213	202,671	163,185

SOURCE: Meltz, 1971b, p. 21

ALTERNATIVE PROJECTIONS OF THE PERCENTAGE DISTRIBUTION OF BACHELOR'S GRADUATIONS BY FIELD OF STUDY IN THE UNITED STATES IN 1981 AND ACTUAL DATA FOR 1961 AND 1969

	Actual		Estimated in 1981	
	1961	1969	A	B
Total graduations	100.00	100.00	100.00	100.00
Natural sciences and related				
Agriculture, engineering, and forestry	10.68	6.82	6.28	5.10
Health professions	6.20	4.35	4.41	3.62
Science	11.72	11.44	11.13	11.99
Social sciences, humanities, and related				
Architecture	0.42	0.45	0.42	0.48
Arts (Letters)	24.57	33.57	33.92	45.26
Education	18.63	15.82	16.90	9.30
Fine arts	3.24	4.55	4.75	5.53
Law	2.37	2.27	2.10	2.03
Music	1.85	1.57	1.62	0.75
Social work	0.68	1.09	1.15	1.99
Other	18.93	17.72	17.10	13.94

NOTE: Percentages may not add to 100 because of rounding.

SOURCE: Meltz, 1971b, p. 20

EARNED DEGREES IN FINE AND APPLIED ARTS[1] CONFERRED BY INSTITUTIONS OF HIGHER EDUCATION, BY LEVEL OF DEGREE AND BY SEX OF STUDENT: UNITED STATES, 1970-71 TO 1977-78

YEAR	BACHELOR'S DEGREES			MASTER'S DEGREES			DOCTOR'S DEGREES		
	TOTAL	MEN	WOMEN	TOTAL	MEN	WOMEN	TOTAL	MEN	WOMEN
1	2	3	4	5	6	7	8	9	10
1970-71	30,394	12,256	18,138	6,675	3,510	3,165	621	483	138
1971-72	33,831	13,580	20,251	7,537	4,049	3,488	572	428	144
1972-73	36,017	14,267	21,750	7,254	4,005	3,249	616	449	167
1973-74	39,730	15,821	23,909	8,001	4,325	3,676	585	440	145
1974-75	40,782	15,532	25,250	8,362	4,448	3,914	649	446	203
1975-76	42,138	16,491	25,647	8,817	4,507	4,310	620	447	173
1976-77	41,793	16,166	25,627	8,636	4,211	4,425	662	447	215
1977-78	40,951	15,572	25,379	9,036	4,327	4,709	708	448	260

1 Includes degrees in fine arts, general; art; art history and appreciation; music (performing, composition, theory); music (liberal arts program); music history and appreciation; dramatic arts; dance; applied design; cinematography; photography; and other fine and applied arts.

SOURCE: U.S. Department of Health, Education, and Welfare, National Center for Education Statistics, Earned Degrees Conferred.

PROFESSIONAL BACKGROUND AND ACADEMIC ACTIVITY OF COLLEGE FACULTY MEMBERS BY TYPE OF INSTITUTION AND BY SEX: UNITED STATES, 1972-73 (IN PERCENTAGES)

MAJOR FIELD OF STUDY: FINE ARTS

ALL INSTITUTIONS			UNIVERSITIES			4-YR COLLEGES			2-YR COLLEGES		
TOTAL	MEN	WOMEN	TOTAL	MEN	WOMEN	TOTAL	MEN	WOMEN	TOTAL	MEN	WOMEN
8.4	8.3	9.2	7.2	7.0	8.4	10.2	9.8	11.2	7.7	8.2	5.9

SOURCE: U.S. Department of Health, Education and Welfare, National Center for Education in the United States; Earned Degrees Conferred and Unpublished Data.

ENROLLMENT FOR ADVANCED DEGREES, BY LEVEL OF ENROLLMENT, SEX OF STUDENT, ATTENDANCE STATUS AND FIELD OF STUDY: UNITED STATES AND OUTLYING AREAS, FALL 1976

FIELD OF STUDY	ALL STUDENTS	TOTAL	FIRST-YEAR STUDENTS					STUDENTS BEYOND THE FIRST YEAR			
			MEN		WOMEN		TOTAL	MEN		WOMEN	
			FULL-TIME	PART-TIME	FULL-TIME	PART-TIME		FULL-TIME	PART-TIME	FULL-TIME	PART-TIME
1	2	3	4	5	6	7	8	9	10	11	12
Enrollment for master's and doctor's degrees:											
Architecture & Environmental Design	10,128	5,933	3,450	852	1,311	320	4,195	2,386	666	888	255
Fine and Applied Arts	30,222	18,472	5,237	3,155	5,286	4,794	11,750	3,669	2,166	3,346	2,569

Students with less than 1 full year of required study for an advanced degree or its equivalent in part-time study.

Students with 1 or more years of required study for an advanced degree.

SOURCE: U.S. Department of Health, Education and Welfare, National Center for Education Statistics, Students Enrolled for Advanced Degrees, Fall 1976

ENROLLMENT FOR MASTER'S AND DOCTOR'S DEGREES, BY FIELD OF STUDY: UNITED STATES AND OUTLYING
AREAS, FALL 1960-FALL 1976

FIELD OF STUDY:		
Fine and Applied Arts	1960	1976
	6,287	30,222

SOURCE: U.S. Department of Education, National Center for Education Statistics, Students Enrolled
by Advanced Degrees

APPENDIX D

BACHELOR'S, MASTER'S AND DOCTOR'S DEGREES CONFERRED IN INSTITUTIONS OF HIGHER EDUCATION BY SEX OF STUDENT, CONTROL OF INSTITUTION AND AREA OF STUDY: AGGREGATE UNITED STATES, 1973-74

	B.A.			M.A.			PH.D.		
	TOTAL	MALE	FEMALE	TOTAL	MALE	FEMALE	TOTAL	MALE	FEMALE
Architecture*	7,840	6,676	1,164	2,773	2,231	502	69	65	4
Public Institutions	5,995	5,216	779	1,730	1,440	290	33	31	2
Private Institutions	1,845	1,460	385	1,003	791	212	36	34	2
Fine and Applied Arts	40,016	15,913	24,103	8,001	4,325	3,676	585	440	145
Public Institutions	23,157	9,246	13,911	5,197	2,848	2,349	345	264	81
Private Institutions	16,859	6,667	10,192	2,804	1,477	1,327	240	176	64

*Includes design

NOTE: There is no B-2 table for 1973-74 and no category for speech and music

SOURCE: National Center for Educational Statistics: Earned Degrees Conferred, 1973-74, U.S. Office of Education, Washington D.C.

BACHELOR'S, MASTER'S AND DOCTOR'S DEGREES CONFERRED IN INSTITUTIONS OF HIGHER EDUCATION BY SEX OF STUDENT, CONTROL OF INSTITUTION AND AREA OF STUDY: AGGREGATE UNITED STATES, 1974-75

	B.A.			M.A.			PH.D.		
	TOTAL	MALE	FEMALE	TOTAL	MALE	FEMALE	TOTAL	MALE	FEMALE
Architecture	4,920	4,489	431	990	865	125	14	9	5
Public Institutions	6,512*	5,428	1,084	1,875	1,509	366	43	37	6
Private Institutions	1,726*	1,375	351	1,078	845	233	26	21	5
Fine and Applied Arts	41,061	15,627	25,434	8,363	4,448	3,915	649	446	203
Public Institutions	24,139	9,350	14,789	5,439	2,887	2,552	390	281	109
Private Institutions	16,922	6,277	10,645	2,924	1,561	1,363	259	163	94

*Includes figures for environmental design

SOURCE: National Center for Educational Statistics: Earned Degrees Conferred, 1974-75

BACHELOR'S, MASTER'S AND DOCTOR'S DEGREES CONFERRED IN INSTITUTIONS OF HIGHER EDUCATION BY SEX OF STUDENT, CONTROL OF INSTITUTION, DISCIPLINE DIVISIONS AND SPECIALTY: AGGREGATE UNITED STATES, 1974-75

	B.A.			M.A.			PH.D.		
	TOTAL	MALE	FEMALE	TOTAL	MALE	FEMALE	TOTAL	MALE	FEMALE
Fine Arts General	5,251	1,864	3,387	779	438	341	51	24	27
Music (Performing)*	4,796	2,155	2,641	2,260	1,235	1,025	228	174	54
Music (Liberal Arts)	3,705	1,657	2,048	732	429	303	110	80	30
Dramatic Arts (includes Speech)	5,467	2,256	3,211	1,348	716	832	92	70	22
All other fields	21,842	7,695	14,147	3,146	1,630	1,616	166	98	70

*Music is divided into performing, liberal arts, history and appreciation. Only the first two categories are listed.

SOURCE: National Center for Educational Statistics: Earned Degrees Conferred, 1974-75, U.S. Office of Education, Washington D.C.

BACHELOR'S, MASTER'S AND DOCTOR'S DEGREES CONFERRED IN INSTITUTIONS OF HIGHER EDUCATION BY SEX OF STUDENT AND DISCIPLINE DIVISION: AGGREGATE UNITED STATES, 1977-78

	B.A.			M.A.			PH.D.		
	TOTAL	MALE	FEMALE	TOTAL	MALE	FEMALE	TOTAL	MALE	FEMALE
Architecture	5,405	4,789	616	1,392	1,519	233	14	12	2
Public Institutions	7,263*	5,612	1,651	1,978	1,493	485	48	37	11
Private Institutions	2,003*	1,455	548	1,143	813	327	25	20	5
Fine and Applied Arts	41,033	15,596	25,437	9,036	4,327	4,709	708	448	260
Public Institutions	24,637	9,589	15,048	5,782	2,802	2,980	404	266	138
Private Institutions	16,396	6,007	10,389	3,254	1,525	1,729	304	182	122

*Includes figures for environmental design

SOURCE: National Center for Educational Statistics: Earned Degrees Conferred, 1977-78, U.S. Office of Education, Washington D.C.

BACHELOR'S, MASTER'S AND DOCTOR'S DEGREES CONFERRED IN INSTITUTIONS OF HIGHER EDUCATION BY SEX OF STUDENT AND BY DISCIPLINE DIVISIONS AND SPECIALTY: AGGREGATE UNITED STATES, 1977-78

	B.A.			M.A.			PH.D.		
	TOTAL	MALE	FEMALE	TOTAL	MALE	FEMALE	TOTAL	MALE	FEMALE
Fine and Applied Arts	41,033	15,596	25,437	9,036	4,327	4,709	708	448	260
Fine Arts General	4,665	1,661	3,004	668	315	353	76	33	43
Music (Performing)*	5,243	2,577	2,666	2,668	1,367	1,301	266	205	61
Music (Liberal Arts)	3,599	1,602	1,997	698	365	333	88	54	34
Dramatic Arts	5,056	2,075	2,981	1,295	659	636	116	80	36
All other fields	22,510	7,681	14,829	3,869	1,783	2,086	162	76	86

*Music is divided into performing, liberal arts and music history. Only the first two categories are listed.

SOURCE: National Center for Educational Statistics: Earned Degrees Conferred, 1977-78, U.S. Office of Education, Washington D.C.

FRESHMAN CHARACTERISTICS AND ATTITUDES

A National Profile Based on Responses of 254,000 Students Who Entered College in Fall, 1983

PROBABLE FIELD OF STUDY

Art, fine and applied: 2.1%

Music: 1.0%

Theater & Drama: 0.6%

OBJECTIVES CONSIDERED ESSENTIAL OR VERY IMPORTANT

Achieving in a performing art:

ALL INSTITUTIONS			2-YR COLLEGES		4-YR COLLEGES				UNIVERSITIES		PREDOMINANTLY BLACK COLLEGES	
MEN	WOMEN	TOTAL	PUBLIC	PRIVATE	PUBLIC	PRIVATE/ NON-SECTARIAN	PROTESTANT	CATHOLIC	PUBLIC	PRIVATE	PUBLIC	PRIVATE
10.5%	13.1%	11.8%	9.2%	13.5%	12.7%	16.5%	13.6%	10.6%	12.1%	16.5%	10.1%	15.1%

SOURCE: The Chronicle of Higher Education; excerpt from the Chronicle Survey, Fact-File, Pg. 13, 1st Issue; Copyright February 1, 1984 by the The Chronicle of Higher Education. Reprinted with Permission.

216

PROFESSIONAL BACKGROUND AND ACADEMIC ACTIVITY OF COLLEGE FACULTY MEMBERS, BY TYPE OF INSTITUTION AND BY SEX: UNITED STATES, 1972-73 (PERCENTAGE DISTRIBUTION)

ITEM	ALL INSTITUTIONS			UNIVERSITIES			4-YR COLLEGES			2-YR COLLEGES		
	TOTAL	MEN	WOMEN	TOTAL	MEN	WOMEN	TOTAL	MEN	WOMEN	TOTAL	MEN	WOMEN
1	2	3	4	5	6	7	8	9	10	11	12	13
Fine Arts	8.4	8.3	9.2	7.2	7.0	8.4	10.2	9.8	11.6	7.7	8.2	5.9

SOURCE: U.S. Department of Education, National Center for Education Statistics, Students Enrolled for Advanced Degrees

217

	ARTS (a)	ALL FIELDS
Number of authorized faculty positions has:		
Increased	9.5%	25.8%
Held steady	61.3%	50.0%
Decreased	28.8%	23.3%
Secretarial and clerical assistance has:		
Increased	7.9%	9.4%
Held steady	62.9%	63.0%
Decreased	25.5%	26.0%
Research and related assistance has:		
Increased	8.7%	9.6%
Held steady	52.5%	46.1%
Decreased	19.9%	32.9%
Funds for faculty travel have:		
Increased	7.9%	9.1%
Held steady	37.2%	34.0%
Decreased	48.7%	53.1%
Funds for faculty leaves with pay have:		
Increased	3.2%	4.8%
Held steady	52.6%	52.5%
Decreased	24.7%	26.6%
Due to changes in personnel, the quality of the department's performance has:		
Substantially improved	12.0%	9.7%
Slightly improved	25.9%	20.6%
Not changed	32.8%	41.2%
Slightly declined	10.3%	12.2%
Substantially declined	3.0%	4.3%
Due to changes in faculty morale the quality of the department's performance has:		
Substantially improved	7.7%	5.7%
Slightly improved	15.8%	13.3%
Not changed	43.0%	36.0%
Slightly declined	18.0%	26.2%
Substantially declined	7.2%	10.8%
Have you been able to attract qualified staff for full-time positions?		
Yes	45.2%	39.4%
Yes, but more difficult	9.9%	15.5%
Yes, but compromised on qualifications	5.2%	8.6%
No, no qualified applicants	3.0%	7.8%
No, unfunded	8.6%	5.4%
No opening	24.1%	21.9%
Do you feel you department is qualified to carry out its mission?		
Yes	39.2%	38.2%
No	57.5%	58.6%
Have you seriously considered leaving in the past two years?		
To go to another university or college	25.4%	24.3%
To take a job outside academe	12.0%	11.5%
To retire early	3.8%	5.3%
No, not seriously	55.0%	57.5%
Faculty control over academic personnel decisions has:		
Increased	4.2%	7.7%
Held steady	63.5%	60.9%
Decreased	22.6%	22.3%

218

	ARTS (a)	ALL FIELDS
Number of course offerings has:		
Increased	34.5%	30.3%
Held steady	47.8%	47.1%
Decreased	16.5%	20.9%
Undergraduate enrollment has:		
Increased	27.1%	42.0%
Held steady	40.2%	34.4%
Decreased	29.9%	20.0%
Graduate enrollment has:		
Increased	12.7%	21.0%
Held steady	25.8%	31.8%
Decreased	18.7%	22.3%
Number of majors has:		
Increased	17.9%	29.2%
Held steady	45.5%	39.4%
Decreased	33.6%	24.0%
Academic prerequisites for majors have:		
Increased	10.4%	14.9%
Held steady	82.8%	76.1%
Decreased	4.6%	4.7%
Library holdings of periodicals in my field have:		
Increased	28.5%	25.2%
Held steady	41.6%	37.6%
Decreased	21.0%	28.5%
Library holdings of books and other media in my field have:		
Increased	48.8%	39.1%
Held steady	33.4%	32.7%
Decreased	13.1%	19.0%
Library services to faculty members have:		
Increased	18.5%	18.1%
Held steady	70.7%	61.3%
Decreased	8.2%	15.1%
Budget for equipment and supplies has:		
Increased	23.6%	21.2%
Held steady	21.0%	30.7%
Decreased	48.2%	42.1%
Replacement and renewal of equipment has:		
Increased	12.8%	13.9%
Held steady	36.9%	41.1%
Decreased	43.7%	37.7%
Maintenance of buildings and facilities has:		
Increased	13.7%	14.1%
Held steady	52.9%	50.4%
Decreased	31.7%	31.3%

(a) Includes architecture, cinema, dance, music and theater

SOURCE: The Chronicle of Higher Education; excerpt from the Chronicle Survey, p. 20 by John Minter Associates; Issue: Copyright November 23, 1983 by the Chronicle of Higher Education. Reprinted with Permission.

Note: Survey data are based on responses from 4,235 faculty members who offered courses from the fall of 1980 through the fall of 1982. To include faculty members newly hired, the sample was drawn from faculty lists that were revised in September, 1982. Data are weighted to represent faculty members at colleges and universities of all types except law and medical schools, proprietary institutions, private two-year colleges, and colleges with fewer than 500 students. Data are also weighted according to the distribution of faculty members in each of eight discipline groups. Technical inquiries about the survey design and sampling techniques should be addressed to John Minter Associates, P.O. Box 107, Boulder, Colorado, 80302.

WEIGHTED NORMS FOR ALL FRESHMEN: FALL 1979
(IN PERCENTAGES)

	ALL INSTITUTIONS	ALL 2-YR COLLEGES	ALL 4-YR COLLEGES	ALL UNIVERSITIES	ALL 2-YR COLLEGES		ALL 4-YR COLLEGES				UNIVERSITIES	
					PUBLIC	PRIVATE	PUBLIC	PRIVATE	PROTESTANT	CATHOLIC	PUBLIC	PRIVATE
FATHER'S OCCUPATION												
Artist including performer	0.80	0.80	0.80	1.00	0.80	0.90	0.80	1.00	0.60	0.60	0.90	1.40
FIELD OF STUDY												
Fine & Applied Arts	1.50	1.50	1.70	1.30	1.40	2.60	1.70	2.50	1.10	0.70	1.60	0.50
PROBABLE CAREER												
Artist	1.30	1.10	1.50	1.00	1.10	2.20	1.50	2.50	1.00	0.50	1.30	0.40
Actor/Entertainer	0.90	0.80	1.10	1.00	0.80	1.00	1.10	0.90	1.30	1.20	0.90	1.20
OBJECTIVE CONSIDERED IMPORTANT												
Achieve in a performing art	10.90	9.40	12.10	11.30	9.10	12.40	11.90	12.30	13.10	11.10	10.90	12.50
Create works of art	11.30	11.00	11.80	10.90	10.70	14.70	11.90	13.30	10.40	9.20	11.10	10.30
STUDENTS WHO PLAYED ON INSTRUMENTS	46.10	38.50	50.00	53.40	37.70	45.20	45.40	55.80	60.00	49.20	52.70	56.20
ATTENDED PUBLIC RECITAL	81.30	75.20	88.10	87.40	74.80	78.70	82.60	88.10	84.80	84.40	86.80	89.70
READ POETRY NOT REQUIRED**												
VISITED ART GALLERY OR MUSEUM**												

**NOT INCLUDED IN 1979 SURVEY

SOURCE: AMERICAN COUNCIL ON EDUCATION: THE AMERICAN FRESHMAN: NATIONAL NORMS FOR FALL 1979

PERCENTAGE DISTRIBUTION OF AMERICAN GRADUATE STUDENTS AMONG ACADEMIC DISCIPLINES, BY SEX

	INTENDED MAJOR FIELD AS ENTERING FRESHMAN			ACTUAL UNDERGRADUATE MAJOR			CURRENT GRADUATE DEPARTMENT			FIELD OF MASTER'S (ACTUAL OR INTENDED)			FIELD OF DOCTORATE (ACTUAL OR INTENDED)		
	MALE	FEMALE	TOTAL	MALE	FEMALE	TOTAL	MALE	FEMALE	TOTAL	MALE	FEMALE	TOTAL	MALE	FEMALE	TOTAL
Architecture and/or design	1.0	0.2	0.7	0.5	0.4	0.2	0.5	0.2	0.4	0.6	0.2	0.4	0.2	0.1	0.2
Fine arts	0.1	0.2	0.1	0.1	0.2	0.2	0.1	0.3	0.2	0.1	0.2	0.2	0.3	0.4	0.3
Art	0.5	2.2	1.0	0.6	2.3	1.2	0.5	1.7	0.9	0.1	0.2	0.2	0.3	0.4	0.3
Dramatics	0.2	1.4	0.6	0.2	1.0	0.5	0.3	0.9	0.5	0.4	0.9	0.6	0.4	1.4	0.6
Speech	0.3	1.3	0.7	0.5	1.0	0.7	0.4	1.5	0.8	0.4	1.6	0.9	0.4	1.2	0.6
Music	1.5	3.3	2.1	1.5	2.6	1.9	1.3	2.1	1.5	1.5	2.2	1.8	1.4	1.9	1.5
Other fine arts	0.1	0.2	0.2	0.2	0.2	0.2	0.2	0.3	0.2	0.2	0.5	0.3	0.2	0.3	0.2

SOURCE: American Council on Education: The American Graduate Student: A Normative Description, Washington, 1971

TABLE E-2
ATTITUDES OF AMERICAN GRADUATE STUDENTS TOWARD HIGHER EDUCATION AND THEIR ACADEMIC EXPERIENCE AND HIGHEST DEGREE EXPECTED (PERCENTAGE DISTRIBUTION)

	ALL GROUPS COMBINED			HIGHEST DEGREE EXPECTED											
				PH.D.			ED.D., D.A., AND OTHER			FIRST PROFESSIONAL			SUBDOCTORAL/NONPROFESSIONAL		
	MALE	FEMALE	TOTAL	MALE	FEMALE	TOTAL	MALE	FEMALE	TOTAL	MALE	FEMALE	TOTAL	MALE	FEMALE	TOTAL
Need for firm undergraduate background in arts & music															
Extremely important	9.5	20.3	13.2	10.2	23.0	13.4	12.8	21.9	15.9	6.4	12.2	7.6	7.6	17.3	12.4
Fairly important	26.0	44.8	32.4	25.8	37.2	28.6	27.8	45.2	33.8	26.9	37.4	29.1	22.1	51.1	36.4
Fairly unimportant	42.6	26.9	37.2	40.1	30.4	37.7	47.2	25.8	39.8	46.2	35.3	43.9	44.1	25.1	34.7
Extremely unimportant	21.9	7.9	17.2	23.9	9.4	20.3	12.2	7.1	10.4	20.5	15.1	19.4	26.2	6.6	16.5

SOURCE: American Council on Education: The American Graduate Student: A Normative Description, Washington, 1971

DEMOGRAPHIC AND BACKGROUND CHARACTERISTICS OF AMERICAN GRADUATE STUDENTS, BY SEX AND HIGHEST DEGREE EXPECTED (PERCENTAGE DISTRIBUTION)

	ALL GROUPS COMBINED			PH.D			E.D., D.A. AND OTHER			FIRST PROFESSIONAL			SUBDOCTORAL/NONPROFESSIONAL		
	MALE	FEMALE	TOTAL	MALE	FEMALE	TOTAL	MALE	FEMALE	TOTAL	MALE	FEMALE	TOTAL	MALE	FEMALE	TOTAL
Attend a concert															
Once a week or more	1.1	1.3	1.1	1.5	1.6	1.5	1.8	1.9	1.8	0.3	0.7	0.4	0.7	1.2	0.9
Two or three times a month	3.9	5.4	4.4	4.2	7.5	5.0	8.2	6.5	7.6	3.0	5.4	3.5	1.6	3.6	2.6
About once a month	11.7	15.9	13.2	13.7	19.2	15.1	11.6	16.9	13.4	12.2	19.2	13.7	7.1	12.9	10.0
A few times a year	43.2	49.9	45.5	44.2	52.2	46.2	40.5	51.9	44.4	46.2	47.0	46.3	39.5	48.9	44.2
Once a year or less	40.1	27.5	35.8	36.4	19.5	32.2	37.9	22.7	32.8	38.4	27.7	36.1	51.1	33.4	42.3
Attend an "art film"															
Once a week or more	1.5	2.1	1.7	1.9	2.1	1.9	0.8	2.3	1.3	1.2	1.6	1.3	0.9	2.1	1.5
Two or three times a month	5.9	7.8	6.5	7.3	11.1	8.2	4.6	9.1	6.1	4.9	7.4	5.4	3.2	5.7	4.4
About once a month	14.8	17.1	15.6	17.0	23.3	18.6	11.3	12.8	11.8	16.9	19.0	17.4	10.5	11.9	11.2
A few times a year	32.4	34.5	33.1	34.5	38.2	35.4	31.7	38.2	33.9	35.5	39.4	36.4	27.5	31.9	29.7
Once a year or less	45.5	38.5	43.1	39.3	25.2	35.9	51.6	37.6	46.8	41.4	32.5	39.5	57.9	48.5	53.2
Attend a play															
Once a week or more	0.4	0.3	0.4	0.4	0.5	0.4	0.4	0.6	0.5	0.4	0.3	0.4	0.3	0.1	0.2
Two or three times a month	2.2	4.1	2.8	2.5	5.6	3.2	2.5	5.1	3.4	2.1	3.3	2.3	1.5	3.5	2.5
About once a month	12.1	18.2	14.2	13.4	21.4	15.4	10.4	19.5	13.5	11.4	18.6	13.0	9.0	14.4	11.7
A few times a year	49.7	55.5	51.7	48.3	53.7	49.7	52.3	57.1	53.9	52.2	60.0	53.9	50.6	57.6	54.1
Once a year or less	35.7	21.8	30.9	35.5	18.9	31.4	34.4	17.7	28.7	33.9	17.8	30.4	38.6	24.4	31.5
Attend an art reception															
Once a week or more	0.8	1.4	1.0	0.7	1.9	1.0	0.7	1.7	1.0	0.8	0.5	0.7	0.9	1.0	0.9
Two or three times a month	2.9	5.1	3.6	3.2	6.3	3.9	3.7	5.5	4.3	2.8	3.0	2.8	1.5	4.1	2.8
About once a month	11.1	15.7	12.7	13.5	20.0	15.2	9.9	15.2	11.7	9.1	15.0	10.4	8.3	13.1	10.7
A few times a year	42.5	49.9	45.1	44.9	50.9	46.4	40.4	53.2	44.8	45.1	52.4	46.7	36.8	49.5	43.2
Once a year or less	42.7	27.9	37.6	37.6	20.9	33.5	45.3	24.4	38.2	42.2	29.1	39.5	52.4	32.3	42.3

SOURCE: American Council on Education: The American Graduate Student: A Normative Description, Washington, 1971

DEMOGRAPHIC AND BACKGROUND CHARACTERISTICS OF AMERICAN GRADUATE STUDENTS, BY FIELDS OF STUDY (PERCENTAGE DISTRIBUTION)

	BIOSCIENCES	BUSINESS	EDUCATION	ENGINEERING	ARTS AND HUMANITIES	MATHEMATICS AND PHYSICAL SCIENCES	SOCIAL SCIENCES	HEALTH FIELDS	LAW
Attend a concert									
Once a week or more	0.5	0.4	0.4	0.5	3.9	1.3	0.6	0.1	0.2
Two or three times a month	3.7	1.8	4.3	3.0	8.1	4.6	3.9	4.2	3.0
About once a month	12.1	9.0	10.1	10.3	19.2	14.1	14.0	13.6	14.2
A few times a year	42.0	44.6	45.5	41.7	46.5	42.2	50.7	47.2	48.5
Once a year or less	41.7	44.2	39.6	44.5	22.3	37.8	30.9	34.9	34.1
Attend an "art" film									
Once a week or more	0.8	0.9	1.0	0.8	4.3	1.4	1.9	0.1	1.1
Two or three times a month	5.1	3.0	4.6	4.4	11.7	5.3	9.5	3.3	6.5
About once a month	12.8	11.1	10.3	11.9	24.2	15.2	20.8	8.8	20.6
A few times a year	31.6	33.4	30.5	30.5	34.6	32.4	36.8	30.3	37.8
Once a year or less	49.8	51.6	53.5	52.4	25.2	45.7	31.0	57.5	34.0
Attend a play									
Once a week or more	0.2	0.4	0.2	0.3	0.9	0.2	0.2	0.0	0.2
Two or three times a month	1.3	2.1	2.9	1.5	5.6	2.2	2.9	1.5	2.5
About once a month	8.0	13.8	13.4	10.2	19.5	10.0	17.8	10.0	15.9
A few times a year	45.7	51.0	53.8	45.7	53.5	48.2	52.7	50.5	54.8
Once a year or less	44.8	32.6	29.7	42.3	20.5	39.5	26.5	38.0	26.5
Attend an art exhibition									
Once a week or more	0.4	0.6	0.6	0.6	3.0	0.3	0.7	0.4	0.8
Two or three times a month	2.1	1.8	3.2	1.9	6.7	2.5	4.9	2.3	3.5
About once a month	11.4	9.2	10.7	9.8	19.1	11.2	14.3	7.0	13.1
A few times a year	43.5	41.9	44.1	39.0	48.3	43.6	49.9	45.2	49.3
Once a year or less	42.7	46.5	41.5	48.6	23.0	42.5	30.3	45.1	33.3

SOURCE: American Council on Education: The American Graduate Student: A Normative Description, Washington, 1971

ESTIMATED FACULTY SALARIES FOR 1983-84

BY TYPE OF INSTITUTION

PUBLIC INSTITUTIONS	Ph.D-granting		Comprehensive		2-year		Total	
	Average (a)	Increase (b)	Average (a)	Increase (b)	Average (a)	Increase (b)	Average (a)	Increase (b)
PROFESSOR	$38,521	5.7%	$34,096	5.0%	$30,606	5.1%	$35,680	5.3%
ASSOCIATE PROFESSOR	29,037	6.0%	27,275	5.1%	27,193	6.1%	28,011	5.7%
ASSISTANT PROFESSOR	24,779	6.4%	22,523	6.5%	22,578	5.2%	23,328	6.1%
ALL RANKS (c)	32,429	5.8%	28,646	5.3%	25,981	5.5%	29,556	5.6%

PRIVATE INSTITUTIONS	Ph.D-granting		Comprehensive		Bachelor's only		Total	
	Average (a)	Increase (b)	Average (a)	Increase (b)	Average (a)	Increase (b)	Average (a)	Increase (b)
PROFESSOR	$43,522	6.6%	$30,492	5.7%	$29,331	7.2%	$33,547	6.5%
ASSOCIATE PROFESSOR	30,109	6.7%	25,026	7.0%	22,165	7.6%	24,772	7.1%
ASSISTANT PROFESSOR	24,945	8.6%	20,946	5.5%	19,163	7.2%	20,291	7.0%
ALL RANKS (c)	34,417	7.1%	25,630	6.1%	22,875	7.3%	26,340	6.8%

BY ACADEMIC DISCIPLINE

PUBLIC INSTITUTIONS

ARTS, FINE & APPLIED	All but 2-year		2-year		Total	
	Average (a)	Increase (b)	Average (a)	Increase (b)	Average (a)	Increase (b)
PROFESSOR	$34,076	5.6%	-	-	$33,169	5.6%
ASSOCIATE PROFESSOR	26,344	5.6%	$28,002	5.6%	26,703	5.6%
ASSISTANT PROFESSOR	21,734	7.8%	-	-	22,610	7.1%
ALL RANKS (c)	28,102	5.9%	26,071	5.2%	27,646	5.8%

PRIVATE INSTITUTIONS

ARTS, FINE & APPLIED	All but 2-year		ALL INSTITUTIONS (Public and Private)	
	Average (a)	Increase (b)	Average (a)	Increase (b)
PROFESSOR	$30,909	3.7%	$31,732	6.3%
ASSOCIATE PROFESSOR	27,619	5.5%	27,038	6.7%
ASSISTANT PROFESSOR	-	-	20,907	7.2%
ALL RANKS (c)	25,207	7.2%	26,189	6.6%

SOURCE: The Chronicle of Higher Education; excerpt from the Chronicle survey by John Minter Associates; Issue; Copyright March 7, 1984 by the Chronicle of Higher Education. Reprinted with Permission.

AVERAGE FACULTY BY SALARIES BY RANK IN SELECTED FIELDS, 1983-84

FIELD	355 PRIVATE INSTITUTIONS						215 PUBLIC INSTITUTIONS					
	PROFESSOR	ASSOCIATE PROFESSOR*	ASSISTANT PROFESSOR*	NEW ASSISTANT PROFESSOR	INSTRUCTOR	ALL RANKS	PROFESSOR	ASSOCIATE PROFESSOR*	ASSISTANT PROFESSOR	NEW ASSISTANT PROFESSOR	INSTRUCTOR	ALL RANKS
FINE ARTS	31,520	25,692	21,025	19,476	17,744	25,755	31,857	24,189	19,950	18,892	16,882	24,046
MUSIC	32,536	26,149	21,698	20,363	18,291	26,076	29,566	23,757	19,430	18,688	16,158	23,476
VISUAL AND PERFORMING ARTS	32,528	26,088	21,289	20,092	17,342	25,899	30,338	24,441	19,913	19,961	17,215	23,464
TOTAL FIELDS	33,552	27,483	22,927	22,245	18,520	27,395	33,776	26,086	21,373	21,023	17,178	26,080

* Includes data for new assistant professors

SOURCE: The Chronicle of Higher Education; excerpt from the Chronicle Survey, College and University Personnel Association; Issue: Copyright February 29, 1984 by the Chronicle of Higher Education. Reprinted with Permission.

APPENDIX E

TENURE INFORMATION

REVIEW POLICY

The College of Arts at a major research university has based
its policy on review procedures for faculty appointment and
promotion in the arts on the following policy statement. They
are given here as information which may be useful to others in
the field. An equivalency is established between research and
artistic creativity; the latter is to encompass original works
and/or creative activities including the production, presentation or performance of works of art. At time a candidate's
contribution may include both research and artistic creativity, as well as bridging the various disciplines of artistic
expression.

Demanded is a special quality for both research and
production, described as distinguished, significant, effective, original or possessing scope, richness and depth. These
terms suggest unique contributions that expand knowledge,
insight and understanding and indicate an imaginative and
innovative mind, as well as the ability to incorporate cre-
tive ideas in actual works or events.

The College also reviewed information supplied by 31
major institutions in the arts across the nation. It
concludes that there is a lack of national agreement concerning the equivalence of scholarly research, artistic creativity and artistic performance as the fulfillment of the
research obligation required under the instruction-research
professorial model such as the one mandated for the University. It concludes that there is a genuine need for fully
articulated review procedures specific to the arts.

The specific thrust of the College's report is the improved incorporation of creative activity and artistic performance within faculty review procedures appropriate to a re-
search-centered university. Although the report makes reference to books, monographs and other publications as evidence
for appointment and advancement, the College found no reason
to recommend a re-structuring of the already well-established
review procedures which presently guide appointment and promotion in such fields as the history, criticism and theory of
music, art, theater, motion picture/television and dance.
Indeed, it is the view of the College that the excellence of
these established procedures for appointment and advancement
has been a principle factor in the development of the high
standards that characterize scholarly research in the arts.
The College commends these procedures and seeks to insure them

in other areas of artistic research, particularly in the performing and creative aspects of the arts, where review procedures, while often quite successful, have been at times controversial or contraproductive.

Some background information will be helpful to place the arts in the context of the university:

The arts are a timeless reflection of every society. The creative artist draws upon the ideas, aesthetics, information, materials and tools at his command and strives to extract the essence of his world and to present it to his community. The scholar, examining these works of art, seeks to document and interpret the artistic expression as well as the society in which it was created. The performer brings artistic works into the reality of contemporary life. The faculty of the College of Arts embraces creative artists, scholars, and performers, and spans the spectrum between them.

A fundamental quality of the arts is their fluidity. The arts change and regenerate, continually evolving in response and reaction to the changes and developments in the human condition, leading to new forms which challenge traditional distinctions within and between the arts.

The arts are by nature experiential, freely engaging intuitive, emotional, unconscious and intellectual processes in their creation and perception. Thus they involve subjective and sometimes contradictory responses, even among groups of artists working in similar fields.

Further, the arts often have no direct utilitarian function. Their value is determined by the manner in which they affect the viewer. Art is a currency of human relationships in which the experience of human beings is joined with the work. The test of artistic excellence may reside in the ability of the work to move an audience--to convince the audience of its own vitality and to expand its awareness. Great works of art and great performances of art accomplish this in qualitatively distinctive ways. Good works of art may achieve this to a lesser degree. Experimental works frequently attempt to sabotage existing feelings, thoughts and perceptions and thereby, to raise new issues and ideas.

The traditional university role as an agency that promotes, supports and encourages free research and experimentation includes the arts in the same sense that it functions in the natural sciences and other fields. In this regard, we must consider university-sponsored performances of theatrical, music, dance works and art exhibits emanating from its faculty as making potentially major contributions to their respective fields. Faculty evaluation in these areas must not diminish the worth of such activities in favor of popular, commercially-funded events and exhibits, thereby promoting safe and non-experimental activities at the cost of artistic freedom.

There must be an understanding that some artists may not choose to participate in the commercial world--or, that they may be rejected by it because of style or a lack of understanding on the part of commercial interests. Sometimes an artist is a failure in the commercial world and a simultaneous success in the academic world. The history of the arts provides numerous examples of good and great artists overlooked or condemned by the taste and judgment of their time.

Considering the diverse and subjective nature of artistic creativity, any judgment in the arts may seem difficult and problematic. However, as in other fields, the most reliable evaluation can be given by the candidate's peers--those engaged in the same type of creativity either within or outside the university (see note 22). Although other persons connected with the arts, such as critics, curators, gallery owners, competition judges and theatrical presenters may contribute meaningful insights, these individuals may also have motivations which do not ensure an unbiased judgment of artistic quality.

It is essential that a depth of expertise be represented in the faculty reviews. In general, careful consultation with peers both within and outside the University is encouraged.

Anonymous

Notes

22 A possible way to think about a systematic peer evaluation procedure for the arts in higher education can be expressed in an arbitrary formula or model: $(T \times W_{ex})^2 \rightarrow A$. T = Talent; W = Work; ex = execution; $()^2$ = chance and the mysterious in the artist's method: A = the art work produced.

APPENDIX F

QUESTIONNAIRE USED FOR FOLLOW-UP STUDY

Institution: _____

Official: _____

Addresses: _____

A PROFILE OF EDUCATION IN THE ARTS IN

INSTITUTIONS OF HIGHER EDUCATION

(This information will be identified with the college - or university - and reported in the ten-year follow-up study of The Rise of the Arts on the American Campus, McGraw-Hill 1973. _____)

Please initial

1. a. The following departments are currently operating: (Please check)

architecture   _____
dance   _____
film   _____
TV   _____
film/TV   _____
music   _____
theater (drama) _____
writing   _____
visual arts   _____
other   _____

  b. The departments listed above are in an administrative unit of: (Please check)

college   _____
school   _____
division _____
other   _____

2. The arts are on administrative unit.

_____yes   _____no

3. a. Number of majors enrolled in all the arts during the Fall of 1982 was _____. In the Fall of 1981 _____. 1980 _____.

Student Majors Enrolled

	Undergraduate			Graduate		
	1980	1981	1982	1980	1981	1982
Architecture						
Dance						
Film						
TV						
Film/TV						
Music						
Theater						
Writing						
Visual arts						
Other						
TOTAL						

Comment? _____

_____

b. In the last five years overall arts enrollment has been: (Please circle)
   1 - up, same, down for majors
   2 - up, same, down for class enrollments

   Please comment: _____

   _____

c. The total number of class enrollments of all students (non-majors and majors) in all classes in the fall quarter (or semester) was:

Undergraduates

	1982-83	1981	1980	1979	1978	
Architecture						
Dance						
Film						
TV						
Film/TV						
Music						
Theater						
Writing						
Visual arts						
Other						

233

	1982-83	1981	1980	1979	1978	
Architecture						
Dance						
Film						
TV						
Film/TV						
Music						
Theater						
Writing						
Visual arts						
Other						

    d. Have you developed an optimal enrollment of majors for each of the arts? _____yes _____no

    e. Do you hold to that enrollment? _____yes _____no
Please comment _____

              _____

4. The arts units in the college are known as (Please circle):
department, school, division, other _____

5. The head of each unit is called (Please circle):
chair, director, head, other _____

6. If there is a dean or director (chief officer for the arts), he reports to: president, vice-president for academic affairs, dean of faculties, provost, others _____

7. a. In the administrative hierarchy of power, budget, and space, the arts are: (Please check)

        (1)-in a respected position   _____
        (2)-so-so
        (3)-barely tolerated   _____
        (4)-threatened   _____
        (5)-on the way out   _____

    b. The arts have risen rapidly on campus over the last 20 years. There has been good support for this rise and there has also been some resistance. This question attempts to identify both support and resistance. If you think the question is not significant or is obscure, circle "0". If resistance has been severe in a given case circle "5" on the resistance side of the scale; if support has been strong, circle "5" on the other side - or whatever seems appropriate, weak to strong, on the 0-5 scale.

234

Strong
Support

Strong
Resistance

The board of trustees (or regents, etc.)

5 4 3 2 1 0 1 2 3 4 5

The chief executive (president, chancellor)

5 4 3 2 1 0 1 2 3 4 5

Chief officer of academic affairs

5 4 3 2 1 0 1 2 3 4 5

Vice-president of business affairs

5 4 3 2 1 0 1 2 3 4 5

Dean of college in which the arts reside

5 4 3 2 1 0 1 2 3 4 5

Academic senate (or other faculty body)

5 4 3 2 1 0 1 2 3 4 5

Student government

5 4 3 2 1 0 1 2 3 4 5

Student body at large

5 4 3 2 1 0 1 2 3 4 5

University curriculum council (if not, please name _____)

5 4 3 2 1 0 1 2 3 4 5

Humanities disciplines

5 4 3 2 1 0 1 2 3 4 5

Social Science disciplines

5 4 3 2 1 0 1 2 3 4 5

Science and math disciplines

5 4 3 2 1 0 1 2 3 4 5

Engineering and technology

5 4 3 2 1 0 1 2 3 4 5

Professional schools (law and medicine)

5 4 3 2 1 0 1 2 3 4 5

School (college) of education

5 4 3 2 1 0 1 2 3 4 5

Alumni association

5 4 3 2 1 0 1 2 3 4 5

Campus business office (purchasing, accounting, etc.)

5 4 3 2 1 0 1 2 3 4 5

Buildings and grounds (maintenance and custodial)

5 4 3 2 1 0 1 2 3 4 5

Alumni (general)

5 4 3 2 1 0 1 2 3 4 5

Alumni in the arts

5 4 3 2 1 0 1 2 3 4 5

Local community

5 4 3 2 1 0 1 2 3 4 5

State Legislature

5 4 3 2 1 0 1 2 3 4 5

Federal agencies

5 4 3 2 1 0 1 2 3 4 5

Private, state and local foundations

5 4 3 2 1 0 1 2 3 4 5

Private national foundations

5 4 3 2 1 0 1 2 3 4 5

Corporations

5 4 3 2 1 0 1 2 3 4 5

Business and merchants

5 4 3 2 1 0 1 2 3 4 5

Arts organizations--commercial and industrial (e.g. graphics, film, TV, music, etc.)

5 4 3 2 1 0 1 2 3 4 5

Idiosyncratic nature of artists-teachers

5 4 3 2 1 0 1 2 3 4 5

Collegiality of faculty

5 4 3 2 1 0 1 2 3 4 5

Other (describe)

5 4 3 2 1 0 1 2 3 4 5

Other (describe)

5 4 3 2 1 0 1 2 3 4 5

8. a. Among the criteria for promotion in your university, is the creative work of your faculty considered equivalent to research in science, social science and the humanitities?

Yes _____ No _____

b. Among the criteria for appointment to the regular faculty is an an academic degree required? Yes _____ No _____; an advanced degree? Yes _____ No _____. If yes, what degree? _____

236

9. Admission for undergraduates to the college (and therefore **one** of its units) or departments in the arts is made:

        _____ a. by university admissions office without recourse to the college or department

        _____ b. by the university admissions in consultation with the college or department

        _____ c. by the college and/or department

        _____ d. by the college after admission to the university

        _____ e. with auditions and/or portfolio plus admissions office

        _____ f. other (please describe) _____

        _____

10. A student major may be dropped from the college or department:

        _____ a. because of lack of talent and/or performance without necessarily referring to grades

        _____ b. because of grades below a certain point

        _____ c. other (please describe) _____

        _____

11. a. Teacher preparation in the arts for kindergarten through twelfth grade is controlled:

        _____ (1) by the college or department

        _____ (2) by the college of education

        _____ (3) by the college or department and the college of education

        _____ (4) other (please describe)

    b. Teacher credentials are awarded after:

        (1) four years _____

        (2) five years _____

        (3) other   _____

12. Recommendation for awarding of the degree is by:

        _____ a. the college and/or department

        _____ b. the college and university requirements

        _____ c. other (please describe) _____

        _____

13. Admission to graduate work is made:

        _____ a. by the graduate college

        _____ b. by the graduate college with recommendation from the college

        _____ c. by the college with recommendation to the graduate college

        _____ d. with auditions and/or portfolio plus graduate college

        _____ e. other (please describe) _____

        _____

14. a. The total college budget or the sum of the budgets of the departments in the arts for the year 1982-83 is: $_____

    b. The budgets for each of the various departments are:

Architecture	$_____	Music	$_____
Dance	$_____	Theater	$_____
Film	$_____	Writing	$_____
TV	$_____	Visual arts	$_____
Film/TV	$_____	Other	$_____

    c. Of the total college budget or sum of the budgets of the departments _____% is for salaries and _____% for operating expenses.

d. The percentages for salaries and operating expenses for each of the various departments are:

Architecture _____ % salaries _____ % operating expenses
Dance _____ % salaries _____ % operating expenses
Film _____ % salaries _____ % operating expenses
TV _____ % salaries _____ % operating expenses
Film/TV _____ % salaries _____ % operating expenses
Music _____ % salaries _____ % operating expenses
Theater _____ % salaries _____ % operating expenses
Writing _____ % salaries _____ % operating expenses
Visual arts _____ % salaries _____ % operating expenses
Other _____ % salaries _____ % operating expenses

e. The university (administration and faculty) understands the peculiar needs of the arts such as space, equipment, time, production funds:

_____ (1) very well
_____ (2) reasonably so
_____ (3) in a vague way
_____ (4) not at all
_____ (5) in a hostile way

15. The budget is prepared:

_____ a. by the dean
_____ b. by the dean in consultation with the chairman of each unit
_____ c. by the dean with the chairman in consultation with chairman of each unit and a faculty (faculty-student) budget committee
_____ d. other (please describe) _____
_____

16. a. Budget hearings are held at the level of vice-president of academic affairs.

Yes _____ No _____ Other (please describe) _____
_____
_____

b. Budget levels for 1982-83 compared to budget levels 1981-82 are about the same _____, higher _____, lower _____.

c. Is the current budget crunch so bad that the effectiveness of teaching, research and public service is seriously impaired?
Yes _____ No _____

d. In the current budget crunch, are the arts being cut more, less, about the same as the other subjects? More _____ Less _____
Same _____

Please comment: _____
_____
_____

17. a. The capital investment for total college buildings or sum of departments in the arts is $_____.

b. The capital investments for each of the various departments are:

Architecture $_____ Music $_____
Dance $_____ Theater $_____
Film $_____ Writing $_____
TV $_____ Visual arts $_____
Film/TV $_____ Other $_____

238

18. a. The total number of square feet for specialized studio and laboratory use (other than general classroom space) in the college or sum of the departments in the arts is _____.

    b. The total number of square feet for each of the various departments are:

       Architecture _____
       Dance   _____
       Film   _____
       TV   _____
       Film/TV   _____
       Music   _____
       Theater   _____
       Writing   _____
       Visual arts _____
       Other   _____

    c. The present plant is effective for current artistic endeavor.
       _____Yes   _____No

    d. We need _____ square feet renovated.

    e. We need _____ additional square feet.

    f. Please elaborate. _____
       _____

19. a. Capital investment for special equipment for the college or sum of departments in the arts is $_____.

    b. Capital investment for special equipment for each of the various departments are:

       Architecture $_____
       Dance $_____
       Film $_____
       TV $_____
       Film/TV $_____
       Music $_____
       Theater $_____
       Writing $_____
       Visual arts $_____
       Other $_____

    c. Needed equipment (not presently available) for optimum operation in the college or sum of the departments in the arts amount to: $_____.

    d. Needed equipment for optimum operation for each of the various departments amounts to:

       Architecture _____
       Dance   _____
       Film   _____
       TV   _____
       Film/TV   _____
       Theater   _____
       Writing   _____
       Visual arts _____
       Other   _____

20. a. Has the administrative structure for arts changed during the last 12 years? Yes_____ No_____. If yes, how? _____
       _____
       _____

    b. If it has not changed, are you satisfied with the present structure? Yes _____ No_____. If no, what structure would you prefer? Please elaborate. _____
       _____
       _____

21. Besides your regular gallery openings, concerts and productions, do you have a special program to bring the arts of the college or of the departments into the mainstream of campus life (dorms, student and faculty centers) by means of events, classes with or without credit, with student and faculty participation?
    Yes _____ No _____
    (Please describe) _____
    _____
    _____
    _____

22. Is the college and/or departments directly involved in the cultural events presented by off-campus artists:

    a. by ex officio members from the college on the "cultural presentations" committee?
       Yes _____ No _____

    b. by directly relating these events to curricular work?

Architecture	_____	Yes	_____	No	
Dance	_____	Yes	_____	No	
Film	_____	Yes	_____	No	
TV	_____	Yes	_____	No	
Film/TV	_____	Yes	_____	No	
Music	_____	Yes	_____	No	
Theater	_____	Yes	_____	No	
Writing	_____	Yes	_____	No	
Visual arts	_____	Yes	_____	No	
Other	_____		_____	Yes	_____ No

    c. Is the cultural program of off-campus artists strictly in the hands of extension services?
       Yes _____ No _____
       Explain: _____
       _____

23. a. Do you feel you have an impact on the surrounding community (residents, schools, business, industry) with your student and faculty artists?
       Strong _____   Weak _____
       Medium _____   None _____
       Comment: _____
       _____

    b. What would you estimate the percentage of attendance is at major on-campus events of the following type:

	Student/Faculty	Community
Architecture	%	%
Dance	%	%
Film	%	%
TV	%	%
Film/TV	%	%
Music	%	%
Theater	%	%
Writing	%	%
Visual arts	%	%
Other	%	%

240

c. Through a formal organization (Friends of the Arts, etc.), do
   you receive financial support from the community?

College	Yes _____	No _____
Architecture	Yes _____	No _____
Dance	Yes _____	No _____
Film	Yes _____	No _____
TV	Yes _____	No _____
Film/TV	Yes _____	No _____
Music	Yes _____	No _____
Theater	Yes _____	No _____
Writing	Yes _____	No _____
Visual arts	Yes _____	No _____
Other	Yes _____	No _____

d. Do you receive outside financial support for the college and the
   departments from:

State arts council	Yes _____	No _____
City arts council	Yes _____	No _____
National Endowment for the Arts	Yes _____	No _____
Foundations	Yes _____	No _____
Individual donors	Yes _____	No _____
Alumni association	Yes _____	No _____
Dept. of Education	Yes _____	No _____
Office of economic opportunity	Yes _____	No _____
Campus research funds	Yes _____	No _____
Other	Yes _____	No _____

e. Total number of arts events (all arts) annually from off-campus
   for which tickets are sold: _____
   Total admissions to arts events from off-campus: _____
   Total income from arts events from off-campus: _____
   Total expenses for arts events from off-campus: _____

f. (1) Do you have a gallery? Yes _____ No _____
       If yes, please continue:

   (2) The gallery is operated by:
       (a) the university _____
       (b) the college _____
       (c) the department of visual arts _____
       (d) other _____

   (3) The director of the gallery serves as a director:
       (a) full time _____
       (b) 3/4 time _____
       (c) 1/2 time _____
       (d) 1/4 time _____
       (e) other _____

   (4) The director has a staff of:
       (a) none _____
       (b) one _____
       (c) two _____
       (d) three _____
       (e) four _____
       (f) more _____

g. If the college or departments offer arts events for which there
   is a charge, the income is deposited to:

   (1) university general funds _____
   (2) a university committee controlling student-faculty arts
       events _____
   (3) student body funds _____
   (4) the college
   (5) the department involved _____
   (6) other _____

h. The college and/or the departments are provided with funds in the
   budget over and above any box office returns to produce arts
   events:
   Yes _____ No _____

i. If yes, the budgets for this purpose annually amount to:

(1) College $_____
(2) Architecture $_____
(3) Dance $_____
(4) Film $_____
(5) TV $_____
(6) Film/TV $_____
(7) Music $_____
(8) Theater $_____
(9) Writing $_____
(10) Visual arts $_____
(11) Other $_____

j. The following undergraduate scholarships and graduate fellowships, teaching and otherwise, are awarded annually:

	Number of undergraduate scholarships	Total amount in dollars	Number of graduate fellowships	Total amount in dollars
Architecture				
Dance				
Film				
TV				
Film/TV				
Music				
Theater				
Writing				
Visual arts				
Other				

24. This is highly subjective, of course, but would you express your feelings as to your departments' (faculty) effectiveness in the following:

a. Contribution of new works in performance and exhibits:
   (1) very effective _____
   (2) moderate _____
   (3) not enough _____
   Comments: _____
   _____

b. Development of an increasingly sophisticated laity (audience_:
   (1) very effective
   (2) moderate
   (3) not enough

c. Exploration of contemporary trends (arts movements):
   (1) very effective
   (2) moderate
   (3) not enough

d. Vital, stimulating exploration of the heritage of each of the arts to introduce the seminal forces of the past:
   (1) very effective
   (2) moderate
   (3) not enough

242

e. Seeking new relationship in the arts:

    (1) very effective
    (2) moderate
    (3) not enough
    Comments: _____

_____

f. Participation in or otherwise supporting his/her professional organization:

    (1) very effective
    (2) moderate
    (3) not enough

25. a. Do you maintain a systematic follow-up study of your graduates in each of the arts? Yes _____ No _____
(Should the university include this as a responsibility of the Office of Institutional Research? Yes _____ No _____)

    b. Are you satisfied with your contribution to the number of "successful" working artists (in the sense of making significant contributions to the various fields professionally)?

        Faculty: Yes _____ No _____
        Student: Yes _____ No _____
        Comments: _____

_____

26. Do you feel your college is having any appreciable effect on the content and procedures of education in the arts in the schools - kindergarten through twelfth grade - in your state?
Yes _____ No _____
(If yes or no, please offer your analysis of this condition.)

_____

_____

_____

27. a. Do you feel that there is, overall, good rapport (rather than a "generation gap") between faculty and students as to the growth and development of each of the fields of the arts?
Yes _____ No _____
Comment: _____

_____

    b. In this regard, is there a growing question of the efficacy of tenure for faculty in the arts in your university?
Yes _____ No _____
Comment: _____

_____

    c. Do your faculty have time for "creative research," pursuing their own work in the arts?
Yes _____ No _____
Comment: _____

_____

    d. How many faculty (full-time FTE), part-time faculty (bodies and sum of all part-time FTE), and student teaching assistants do you have in each of the arts? (see next page)

243

	Number or full-time faculty FTE	Number of part-time faculty (bodies)	Sum of all FTE's	Number of students teaching asst.
Architecture				
Dance				
Film				
TV				
Film/TV				
Music				
Theater				
Writing				
Visual arts				
Other				
Other				

Comment: _____

_____

28. Do you believe in and have evidence, to your satisfaction, of a growing surge of interest and pursuit of the arts in:
    a. your student majors: Yes _____ No _____
    b. the general student body: Yes _____ No _____
    Comment: _____

    _____

29. Do you have any impression, hunch, or hard evidence that educating students will demand more technological equipment or that a trend is toward the simpler, more humanized technologies? For example, synthetic sound vis-a-vis the guitar, mechanized theatres vis-a-vis street theatre, or ecumenical communal arts living groups (Bread-and-Puppet Theatre) vis-a-vis the heavy budget demanding centers (Lincoln Center)?
    a. Technology-oriented _____
    b. Simple, humanized approach _____
    c. Both are required _____
    Comment: _____

    _____

30. Please make any further statement and suggestions here. (For example: Have any key aspects of the arts been omitted? What of the above do you consider inconsequential?)

    _____
    _____
    _____
    _____
    _____
    _____
    _____
    _____
    _____
    _____
    _____

(Please use back of page.)

Return to: Dr. Jack Morrison, College of Fine Arts, UCLA, Los Angeles, CA 90024

244

About the Author

Something of a maverick in academe, Dr. Jack Morrison was a founding member of the Department of Theater Arts at UCLA in 1947. This was before he received an advanced degree in 1952 at UCLA. There he directed the U.S. premiere of Albert Camus,' The Just, and introduced one of the first university courses in theater management and administration. He took an Ed.D. at the University of Southern California in 1962.

Invited to take the Deanship of the College of Fine Arts at Ohio University (Athens, Ohio) in 1966, the author also was a theater and dance specialist for the then Office of Education in 1964-65. He kept working his way east by becoming the Associate Director of the Arts in Education Program at the John D. Rockefeller 3rd Fund in New York City in 1971--and then to Washington D.C. in 1976 as Executive Director of the American Theatre Association. Upon retirement in 1982, Morrison returned to his native Southern California, joined the staff of the UCLA College of Fine Arts and wrote this book as a follow-up of the study he did for Clark Kerr's Commission on Higher Education which McGraw-Hill brought out in 1973 as The Rise of the Arts on the American Campus.

FIGURE LEGENDS

FIGURE 1. The Paul Green Theatre. Opened in 1981 on the campus of the University of North Carolina, Chapel Hill. A thrust stage, seating 504, the Paul Green Theatre is one of two theaters operated by Playmakers Repertory Company and the Department of Dramatic Art. (Insert photo on pg. 17.)

FIGURE 2. Aerial view of Bennington College with Arts Center in foreground: (a) Lester Martin Drama Workshop, (b) Martha Hill Dance Workshop, (c) Susan A. Greenwall Music Workshop. (photo by Alex Brown.) (Insert photo on pg. 127.)

FIGURE 3. College of Fine Arts Building, Carnegie-Mellon University. (Insert photo on pg. 130.)

FIGURE 4. Hopkins Center, Dartmouth College. (photo by Stuart Bratesman.) (Insert photo on pg. 135.)

FIGURE 5. Model of new Hood Museum at Dartmouth College. Hopkins Center (on right) connects to Museum by arched passageway in center of photo. (photo by Stuart Bratesman.) (Insert photo on pg. 136.)

FIGURE 6. Frederick D. Hall Music Center, Jackson State University. (Insert photo on pg. 158.)

FIGURE 7. Schoenberg Hall Music Building, University of California, Los Angeles. (Insert photo on pg. 176.)

FIGURE 8. Dickson Art Center at University of California, Los Angeles. Houses classrooms and offices of the art department as well as galleries which have housed major exhibitions. (Insert photo on pg. 177.)

FIGURE 9. The Elena Baskin Visual Arts facility on the University of California, Santa Cruz campus. (Insert photo on pg. 183.)

FIGURE 10. Fine Arts Building, University of Georgia. (Insert photo on pg. 188.)